The Relaxed Businessman

GST & Income Tax Made Simple
make your business a GIFT, Not a BURDEN

A SIMPLE GUIDE TO GST, INCOME TAX, AND CHOOSING THE RIGHT PROFESSIONAL

By

Adv DEEPAK CHHABRA

WHY THIS BOOK?

Agenda for writing the books:

As a result of my work over the past ten years with numerous businesspeople, I am aware of the various accounting concepts and direct and indirect tax rules that a businessman must adhere to in his day-to-day operations. Nevertheless, he frequently commits the same errors. Later, when he is under audit, investigation, etc., these things throw his life into chaos.

I therefore decided to give them a couple of the errors along with information that will aid them in managing their business.

Then what will be mentioned in this book?

I am aware that you are eager to learn about mistakes, including instances from real life, and how we can prevent them.

ABOUT THE AUTHOR

Adv Deepak Chhabra is a taxation advocate and a commerce graduate. He qualified as an LL.B. in 2014 and has been in practice since 2015.

Deepak has had the privilege of consulting various industries on taxation, GST, and financial reporting.

With experience, he now specializes in providing GST and Income Tax Services, simplifying them for businesses so they can grow without hiccups and fear of taxes.

He aims to spread awareness about the benefits of compliance and how it can become a company's growth accelerator.

Deepakk Chhabra & Associates ®

DC x Classes™

Adv Deepak Chhabra

advocatedeepak13@gmail.com

+91 91157-15359

Office: +91 77176-00901

ACKNOWLEDGEMENT

As an avid reader and lifelong learner, writing a book had been on my bucket list for years, but I lacked motivation.

One day, I realized I had a unique perspective to share with the world that could make a difference.

My Mentor, Mr. Gaurav, and my family helped me stay focused on my goals, held me accountable for my progress, and provided valuable feedback on the content and structure of my book. Without their guidance, I would not have been able to complete my book.

The support of my family and my mentor helped me overcome setbacks and obstacles. Their unwavering belief in me was a powerful motivator. They reminded me of my strengths and capabilities when I doubted myself. My mentor provided accountability, which was a critical factor in keeping me on track and focused on my goals.

Deepakk Chhabra & Associates [®]

DC x Classes [TM]

Adv Deepak Chhabra

advocatedeepak13@gmail.com

+91 91157-15359

Office: +91 77176-00901

DISCLAIMER

This is a work of fiction. names, characters, businesses, places, events and incidents are either the products of the author's imagination or used fictitiously. Any resemblance to actual persons, living or dead, or actual events is purely coincidental.

TABLE OF CONTENTS

GST INTRODUCTION

GST: Goods and Services Tax

GST was implemented on **01.07.2017**.

➢ Supplying goods/services **within the same state (local supply)** is called **Intra-State Supply**, and **CGST and SGST** are applicable.

➢ Supplying goods/services **to another state (outside the state)** is called **Inter-State Supply**, and **IGST** is applicable.

General Portal:www.gst.gov.in

E-Way Bill Generation Portal:www.ewaybillgst.gov.in

Invoice Registration Portal [IRP]: www.einvoice1.gst.gov.in

Full Form of GSTIN: Goods and Services Tax Identification Number

GST REGISTRATION

Threshold Limits for Registration

➢ For Supply of Goods: ₹40 lakhs

➢ For Supply of Services: ₹20 lakhs

➢ *(In some special category states, the limits are ₹20 lakhs for goods and ₹10 lakhs for services.)*

If a person is dealing only in tax-free/exempted supplies, GST registration is not required.

If Supplying Both Taxable Goods and Services

The threshold limit becomes ₹20 lakhs, and GST registration becomes mandatory once this limit is crossed.

Example:

If Daiwik supplies:

➢ Taxable goods worth ₹5 lakhs

➢ Services worth ₹2 lakhs

➢ Nil-rated (tax-free) supplies worth ₹60 lakhs

Then, GST registration is still compulsory because a taxable supply (₹7 lakhs) exists.

Deadline For Registration

Once you become liable for GST registration, you must apply within 30 days.

Types of GST Registration

➢ Regular Registration

➢ Composition Scheme

Documents Required for GST Registration

➢ PAN Card

➢ Aadhaar Card

➢ Passport-size photograph

➢ Ownership proof (e.g., property registry, electricity bill)

➢ Rent agreement (if the premises are rented)

➢ Photo of the business location with name board (from GPS-enabled camera)

➢ Email ID and mobile number

➢ Partnership deed (for partnership firms)

Additional Place of Business

➢ If you have a godown, register it as an Additional Place of Business.

> If you have branches in the same state, add them under the same GST number (if you are not taking a separate GSTIN).

Note:

You can have unlimited branches/godowns under one GSTIN within the same state, or you may choose to apply for separate GST numbers.

This decision is up to the business owner.

Inter-State Operations

If you are doing business in another state, a separate GST number for that state is mandatory.

PRECAUTIONS AFTER GETTING A GST NUMBER

➢ When you receive a GST number, it comes with three pages. Keep a set of these three pages at both the **Principal Place of Business** and any **Additional Places of Business**.

The **first page** of the GST certificate should be **framed and displayed in the office of the Principal Place of Business (shop/showroom)**.

If you are registered under the **Composition Scheme**, you must also display the following line:

"Composite Taxable Person Not Eligible to Collect Tax on Supply"

➢ It is **mandatory** to display the **firm name, GST number, and complete address** outside your premises.

This display must remain even if the shop/showroom is closed (like on Sundays or at night).

If you are a **Composition Dealer**, you must also display the following line:

"Composite Taxable Person Not Eligible to Collect Tax on Supply"

➢ Your Principal Place of Business must have:

- All bill books

- Stock registers

- A computerized system

These are **basic and compulsory documents**. Further details are explained separately.

Note: The GST User ID and Password must be provided by both theprofessional and the business owner.

INVOICE FORMAT (AS PER GST LAW)

Every invoice must comply with the GST rules. There are different types of invoices, such as:

- Tax Invoice

- Bill of Supply

- Invoice-cum-Bill of Supply

- Revised Tax Invoice

- Credit Note

- Debit Note

- And others

Mandatory Fields on an Invoice:

- GSTIN of the supplier and recipient (if applicable)

- Invoice number

- Invoice date

- Place of supply

- Description of goods/services

- HSN/SAC code

> Quantity

> Unit

> Value of goods/services

> Applicable taxes

Key Requirements:

> Issuing an invoice is mandatory for every supply.

> If the invoice amount exceeds ₹50,000, generating an E-Way Bill is required.

> If the turnover exceeds five crores, then E-Invoicing is mandatory.

Note:

If your supply is below ₹200, and the customer does not demand a separate invoice, then you can issue a consolidated invoice for the entire day's small supplies.

Example:

Customers made purchases of ₹150, ₹180, ₹80, ₹60, ₹50, ₹10 (Total = ₹530).

Instead of individual invoices, you can issue one consolidated invoice at the end of the day.

Types of Invoices and Notes:

Tax Invoice

➤ Used for taxable goods/services.

➤ Issued when a registered supplier supplies goods to a registered recipient.

Bill of Supply

➤ When a registered supplier supplies exempt goods/services

➤ By a composition dealer

Copies Required:

For Goods (3 copies):

➤ Original – for the recipient

➤ Duplicate – for transporter

➤ Triplicate – for the supplier

For Services (2 copies):

➤ Original – for the recipient

➤ Duplicate – for the supplier

Debit Note

- ➤ Issued by the supplier.

- ➤ No time limit for issuing.

- ➤ Issued when:

  - o There's an error in the original invoice (e.g., undercharged tax or value)

- ➤ The format is similar to an invoice.

- ➤ Mentioning GSTIN is mandatory.

Credit Note

- ➤ Issued by the supplier to the recipient in cases such as:

  - o Sales returns

  - o Overcharged tax or value

- ➤ Must be issued on or before 30th November of the next financial year.

GST RETURN

There are two types of GST registrations – Regular and Composition. Let's first talk about the Regular GST Number.

REGULAR REGISTRATION

When we take a regular GSTIN, you are required to file two main types of returns:

1. GSTR-1

2. GSTR-3B

> If your turnover is up to ₹5 crores, you can file returns quarterly.

> If your turnover is more than ₹5 crores, you must file monthly.

Due Dates for Regular Returns

Return Type	Monthly Due Date	Quarterly Due Date
GSTR-1	11th	13th
GSTR-3B	20th	22nd/24th

Late Fees & Interest:

> GSTR-3B: ₹50 per day (₹25 CGST + ₹25 SGST)

> GSTR-3B (Nil Return): ₹20 per day (₹10 CGST + ₹10 SGST)

- GSTR-1: ₹200 per day (₹100 CGST + ₹100 SGST) **Note:** Currently, GSTR-1 late fees are not being charged, but some states have issued penalty notices.

- If you delay filing and tax is payable, interest at @18% must be paid.

- If a return is not filed for a month, you cannot file the next month's return until the previous one is filed.

Important Advice:

Try to submit all data to your tax consultant by the 2nd or 3rd of the month so they can file GSTR-1 on time (preferably by the 7th).

Filing GSTR-1 on time ensures that your recipient (purchaser) can see it in GSTR-2B by the 14th and claim ITC in the same month.

If you file late, the buyer may not be able to claim ITC, possibly leading to an extra tax burden and loss of trust, which could result in future business loss.

Return Filing Status Check:

You can verify if a party is filing GST returns on time:

- Visit: www.gst.gov.in

- Go to: Search Taxpayer → Search by GSTIN/UIN

- Scroll down to check the return filing status (GSTR-1, GSTR-3B, GSTR-9, etc.)

Tip:

Before purchasing from any vendor, check their GST return filing history. A supplier who files on time is more reliable.

GSTR-1:

In GSTR-1, you upload sales details, including:

➢ B2B (Business-to-Business)

➢ B2C (Business-to-Consumer)

➢ Exempted sales

➢ HSN codes (product/service classification)

GSTR-2B:

When your supplier files their GSTR-1 on time, your GSTR-2B gets updated by the 14th.

GSTR-2B contains:

➢ Eligible ITC (Input Tax Credit)

➢ Ineligible ITC

GSTR-3B:

Includes:

➢ Total sales value

➢ RCM (Reverse Charge – e.g., Freight)

➢ ITC, as per GSTR-2B

The benefit of early filing: Filing GSTR-1 on time helps recipients claim ITC promptly.

GSTR-9 (Annual Return)

➢ Annual return showing total sales, ITC, RCM, and taxes for the whole year.

➢ If any tax is payable, pay it with interest.

➢ If you forgot to claim ITC on any bill, you can claim it by 30th November of the next financial year.

➢ Mandatory for businesses with a turnover of over ₹2 crores.

➢ It must be filed carefully.

COMPOSITION REGISTRATION

➢ Available for businesses with turnover up to ₹1.5 crores (₹75 lakhs for special category states).

➢ For professionals, if receipts are upto ₹50 lakhs, they can opt for composition.

Special Category States:

Nagaland, Manipur, Tripura, Mizoram, Sikkim, Uttarakhand, Meghalaya, Arunachal Pradesh

Returns for the Composition Scheme:

1. GSTR-4 – Annual return (sales & purchase details for the year)

2. CMP-08 – Quarterly statement (to be filed every quarter)

Tax Rates under composition: 1%, 5%, or 6% (varies by business type)

➤ Taxes are to be paid quarterly

➤ Late filing attracts 18% interest

GSTR-4 Due Date: 30th June after the end of the financial year.

This scheme is ideal for small businesses, especially those selling directly to end consumers.

INPUT TAX CREDIT (ITC)

ITC is a core (main) part of the GST system.

If you claim ITC when it is not eligible, you may receive a notice from the GST Department.

On the other hand, if ITC is eligible, but you are also supplying exempt goods and still claim full ITC, you can also receive a notice.

Simplified Conditions to Claim ITC:

➢ The recipient must have a valid tax invoice.

➢ The supplier must have filed the GST return.

➢ The recipient must receive the goods.

Important Notes:

➢ **Composition Dealer:** Cannot claim ITC.

➢ **Regular Dealer:**

- If supplying only taxable goods, you can claim ITC on goods and packing materials.

- If supplying only exempt goods, no ITC is allowed (not even on packing material).

- If taxable and exempt goods are supplied, ITC will be allowed on a proportional basis (including packing material).

- If full ITC is claimed, it must be reversed with interest.

Example: If you install an air conditioner:

- If you make only taxable sales, you can claim the full ITC.

- If you sell only exempt goods, no ITC is allowed.

- If you deal in both, you must calculate the eligible ITC every month based on the turnover ratio.

Time Limit to Claim ITC:

You can claim ITC within the same period, up to 30th November of the next financial year, or before filing the annual return, whichever is earlier.

ITC on Motor Vehicles – Generally Not Allowed, but allowed if:

- Used for the further supply of such vehicles

- Used for the transportation of passengers

- Used for training in driving, flying, or navigation

- Used for the transportation of goods

No ITC Allowed On:

Food & Beverages, Outdoor Catering, Treatment, Cosmetic or Plastic Surgery, Health Services – except when you are providing the same services (i.e., same supply)

Works Contract Services:

The work contract includes construction, fabrication, installation, maintenance etc., related to immoveable property.

- If a contractor provides the same service further, they can claim ITC.

- If you are building your own factory/shop/house, no ITC is allowed on construction expenses.

Other Situations Where ITC Is Not Allowed:

- If goods are used for personal use.

- If goods are purchased from a composition dealer.

- If goods are lost, stolen, destroyed, or given as free samples or gifts.

AMENDMENT

➤ If you want to change your email ID and mobile number, you can do so within 15 minutes.

➤ If you change the Principal Place of Business, any godown, or any branches, you must inform the GST Portal within 30 days.

➤ You can convert from Regular registration to Composition registration and also from Composition registration to Regular registration.

➤ You can also change the name of the firm/trade name.

➤ If yours is a partnership firm, you can also add or remove partners.

COMMON MISTAKES MADE BY BUSINESSMEN WHILE MAKING PURCHASES

In this chapter, I want to tell you a few areas where you should focus while purchasing goods/services:

1. Not Checking GST Return Filing Status

Before purchasing goods, always check the GST return filing status of the supplier using their GSTIN.

➢ If the supplier files returns on or before the due date, they are considered compliant.

If the supplier files after the due date, you may not get an Input Tax Credit (ITC) in the same month.

This can affect your working capital and may even lead to GST notices later.

Author's Note: Based on my experience, if a supplier files March's return after the last date despite filing other returns on time, it may indicate bogus billing. Avoid purchasing from such dealers.

2. Monthly vs. Quarterly Return Filing

➢ If the supplier files monthly returns, your ITC reflects monthly, which is ideal.

➢ If they file quarterly returns, your ITC will be delayed, and you might have to pay tax upfront.

Suggestion: Ask quarterly filers to use **IFF** (Invoice Furnishing Facility), a monthly option for reporting B2B invoices, so that your ITC shows up in GSTR-2B monthly.

3. Payment Not Made Within 180 Days

➢ According to the GST law, payment must be made within 180 days from the invoice date.

➢ If not, you are required to reverse the ITC and only reclaim it after making payment.

Example:

Invoice = ₹590 (₹500 + ₹90 GST)

If you pay only ₹295 (50%), you can claim only ₹45 ITC proportionately.

4. Not Verifying Invoice Details Properly

Often, GSTIN is incorrectly entered on the invoice.

Example:

➤ Correct GSTIN: 03AATPM2643A1ZG

➤ Entered by mistake: 03AATPM2643IZG

This error causes the invoice to not appear in GSTR-2B, and you will lose ITC eligibility.

5. **Tax Must Be Shown Separately on the Invoice**

Ensure the invoice shows tax separately (CGST, SGST, or IGST).

This allows easy matching with GSTR-1 and helps claim accurate ITC.

6. **Buying from a Composition Dealer**

Check online whether the supplier is Regular or Composition.

➤ Composition dealers cannot charge GST, and you cannot claim ITC on such purchases.

➤ If you claim ITC by mistake, you'll have to pay tax when reselling those goods.

7. **Invoice without GSTIN**

If the supplier does not mention GSTIN on the invoice, you cannot claim ITC.

8. **Incorrect Place of Supply**

Always verify the Place of Supply mentioned in the invoice.

➢ If it is incorrectly shown for another state, the wrong tax might be applied, and penalties can follow

☑ How to Check a GST Number (GSTIN)

To verify whether a dealer is Regular or Composition and whether they've filed returns:

1. Visit: https://services.gst.gov.in/services/searchtp

2. Enter the GSTIN of the supplier

3. Fill in the CAPTCHA

4. Click Search

You'll be able to see:

➢ Type of registration (Regular or Composition)

➢ Return filing status

➢ Last return filed

➢ Contact details

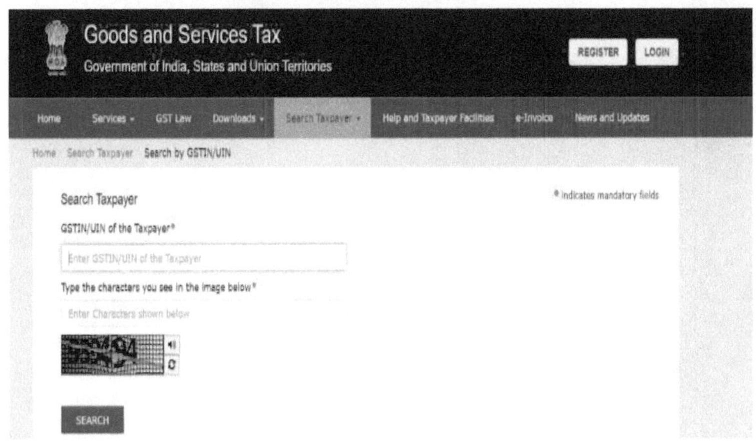

Then scroll down and click on show filling table as below:

HSN: Harmonized System of Nomenclature of Goods and Services

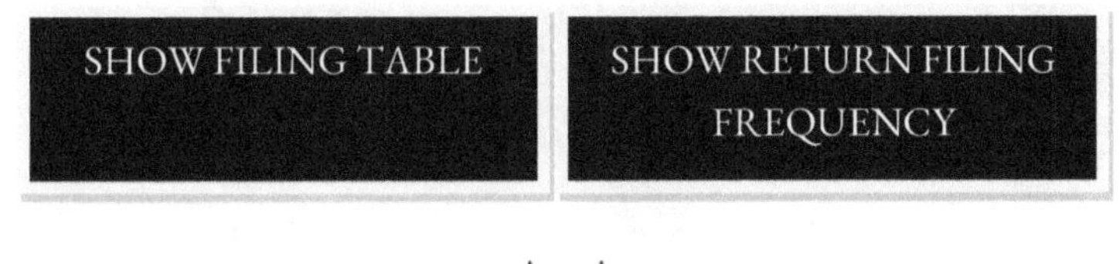

★ ★ ★ ★

MISTAKES WHILE MAKING A SALE

1. Missing the Buyer's GST Number:

Many times, the buyer shares their GST number through WhatsApp or email, but the seller forgets to mention it on the invoice while billing. As a result, the sale gets uploaded as B2C (Business-to-Consumer) instead of B2B (Business-to-Business) in the GSTR-1 return.

When this is noticed later, the seller has to amend the GSTR-1 return, which can be problematic. Sometimes, this issue is identified two years later, by which time the amendment window has already closed, creating complications in claiming the Input Tax Credit (ITC) for the buyer.

2. Entering the Wrong GST Number:

Business owners or accountants often accidentally enter the wrong GSTIN, especially when dealing with firms with similar names. This issue typically comes to light only during audits.

Example:

Doomra Karyana Store sold goods to M/s Chhabra Trading Co., but due to a mistake, the GST number of Chhabra Traders (a different entity) was entered instead.

3. GST on Advance Payments (for Services):

If you provide services and receive an advance payment, you must pay GST on that advance.

GST is applicable based on the earliest of the following events:

- Date of receipt of the advance

- Date of invoice generation

- Date of actual supply of the service

COMMON MISTAKES THAT LEAD TO GST NOTICES

➢ Mismatch in Sales between GSTR-1 and GSTR-3B.

➢ Differences between the audited balance sheet and GST returns.

➢ Non-payment of tax under the Reverse Charge Mechanism (RCM).

➢ Excess ITC claimed in GSTR-3B compared to the lower ITC reflected in GSTR-2A and GSTR-2B.

➢ If payment to creditors is not made within 180 days, the ITC must be reversed. Failure to do so can result in a GST notice.

➢ If tax is payable in GSTR-3B but the return is filed after the due date without paying interest, a notice may be issued.

➢ Mismatch in sales and ITC figures across GSTR-9, GSTR-9C, GSTR-3B, and GSTR-1.

➢ In works contract cases, if a government department deducts TDS on payment, and the taxpayer files the TDS return and accepts it but shows a lower supply amount in GSTR-1,a GST notice can be issued.

- *(For contracts above ₹2,50,000, government departments deduct TDS at 1% CGST and 1% SGST)*

- **Example:** If PWD makes a payment of ₹5,00,000 to a contractor, they may deduct ₹5,000 CGST and ₹5,000 SGST. If the taxpayer accepts the TDS and it reflects in the cash ledger but reports only ₹3,00,000 as supply in GSTR-1, the discrepancy may lead to a notice.

➢ If the invoice (bill) format is not as per legal requirements, and any person uploads it on a government app(Mera Bill App), a GST notice can also be issued.

HOW TO CHOOSE THE RIGHT PROFESSIONAL

Every businessman must maintain Books of Accounts, which requires hiring a professional. However, choosing the right professional can be difficult.

If you choose the right professional, you can not only **grow your business** but also **avoid potential notices** from tax authorities. A good professional will help you generate value and make your business more secure.

Important Tips for Choosing the Right Professional

Don't entrust all your work to a single person—whether it's a CA, CS, Advocate, or Accountant. If one person is handling everything, they might miss identifying errors in your accounts, as they will be overburdened with tasks. This could lead to problems down the line, including improper tax filings.

Best Approach: Hire Separate Professionals

It's better to hire an accountant separately to handle your sales and purchase entries, as well as bank transactions. In addition, hire a taxation professional (like an Advocate, CA, or CS) to manage your tax returns and ensure everything is in order.

By having two professionals(an Accountant and a Taxation Professional), you will:

➤ Do not depend on a single person for everything.

➤ Consult both professionals for different aspects of your business.

➤ Increase your security and reduce the chances of receiving tax notices.

Fees and Benefits

While the fees for two professionals may be divided, you will still be paying the same total amount you would have paid to a single person. The advantage is that **your books will be properly checked**, and your tax returns will be more accurate. With two separate professionals, you get better overall attention to detail.

A single person handling everything may focus only on **clerical tasks** and might not keep up with regular updates and amendments in the law. This could lead to errors, and you might miss out on important changes in taxation laws.

Why Separate Professionals?

➤ **Specialization**: A taxation professional (like a CA or advocate) will focus on regular amendments to the tax laws. They will attend seminars, stay updated, and have time to study changes.

➤ **Avoid Overburdening**: A person handling multiple areas, like GST, Income tax, EPF, loans, and more, might not have the time or capacity to stay up-to-date with all the changes. It's important to hire professionals who specialize in specific areas, just like you would choose a specialized doctor for your health issues.

By hiring professionals who specialize in areas like GST and Income Tax, you will have a **more secure future**, and the chances of getting notices from tax authorities will be significantly reduced. You'll also be financially stronger and more prepared for any future audits.

Regular Communication with Your Professionals

➤ **Call your Taxation professional regularly**: When your accountant sends the returns to the taxation professional, ensure that you consult your Consultant or visit the office regularly.

➤ **Quarterly Reviews**: At least once every three months, meet with your taxation professional to check your books, inquire about any amendments in the law, and review your stock, ITC, and overall records.

➤ **Six-Monthly Reviews**: Prepare a provisional balance sheet every six months and review your Trading Account, Profit & Loss (P&L), and Balance Sheet. This is a **symbol of growth** and ensures that you won't face problems with the taxation department **or** when applying for a loan from the bank.

By following these steps, you can ensure the smooth functioning of your business, avoid tax issues, and be in a **strong financial position**.

DOCUMENTS DEPARTMENT REQUIRES YOU TO MAINTAIN

Every registered person is required to maintain books of accounts for 72 months, i.e., 6 years from the date of filing of the Annual Return or 1 year from the date of finalization of appeal, investigation, etc.

1. **Records to be kept by manufacturer:-**

    - Production Register

    - Sale, Supply Register

    - ITC Register

    - Output Tax Paid Register

    - Import and Export Register

    - Stock Register

    - Quantitative details of the goods manufactured

    - Purchase Register

2. **Records to be kept by traders:-**

    - Purchase Register

    - Sale/Supply Register

- ➢ ITC Register

- ➢ Output tax paid register

- ➢ Stock Register

- ➢ Import and export Register

3. Records to be kept by Service Provider:-

- ➢ Purchase Register

- ➢ Sale/supply Register

- ➢ ITC Register

- ➢ Output tax paid Register

- ➢ Import and Export Register

4. Record to be kept by Warehouse operators or Transporters:-

- ➢ Records of goods transported, delivered, and stored in transit

- ➢ Books for goods receipts, dispatched, moved, and disposed of

- ➢ Store goods to identify item-wise and owner-wise.

Along with the following documents, a businessman is required to keep:

- ➢ Records relating to supplies attracting Reverse charges along with their document, i.e., bill of supply, delivery challans, credit notes, debit notes, e-way bills, etc.

> Records for advances received and paid, as well as details of their adjustments in invoices, are also included.

> Complete addresses of the suppliers and recipients.

> Complete address of the premises where he stores the goods.

If the books of accounts are not maintained properly under GST by the GST-registered person, there is a minimum penalty of ₹ 20000/-.

GST REFUND

If there is a balance in the **cash ledger**, then the refund will be granted.

In the case of **ITC (Input Tax Credit)**, generally, two types of refunds are available:

➤ **Export (Zero-Rated Supply)**

➤ **Inverted Duty Structure**

Inverted Duty Structure: In this case, the tax rate on **output supply/sale** is lower, and the tax rate on **input (purchase)** is higher.

For example: The output tax (on sale) on an e-bike is 5%, but the battery used in it is taxed at 28%.

FOCUS ONLY ON BUSINESS

In the previous chapter, we discussed the importance of having a **Good Professional**. If you choose the **right professional**, you can avoid unnecessary **litigation** and ensure **steady growth** in your business. A skilled professional doesn't just manage compliance — they **generate value** for your business.

So, you should **focus solely on running your business**.

My advice:

➢ Choose a competent and reliable professional.

➢ This will not only boost your business growth but also help you generate better income and manage time more efficiently.

WHY SHOULD I PAY TAXES?

Taxes are often perceived as an obligation, a financial burden imposed by the government. However, in reality, taxes are the foundation of a nation's progress and prosperity. Every rupee paid as Tax contributes to building roads, enhancing national security, improving healthcare, and uplifting the underprivileged.

Paying taxes is not merely a legal duty; it is a civic responsibility that fuels the development of the country. The government uses the Tax for:

Building Infrastructure and Public Services

Strong infrastructure is the backbone of any developed nation. Taxes fund the highways we travel on, the bridges we cross, and the railways that connect distant regions. Taxes also support public services such as fire departments, disaster management, and waste disposal systems, ensuring a safer and cleaner environment for all citizens.

The Delhi-Mumbai Expressway, one of India's largest highway projects, is financed through public funds, including taxes. Similarly, metro expansions in cities like Bengaluru, Mumbai, and Chennai are made possible through tax revenue.

Funding Government Schemes and Social Welfare Programs

Taxes serve as the financial backbone of various government welfare schemes, which aim to improve the quality of life for millions.

From healthcare and employment programs to financial inclusion initiatives, taxes help bridge the gap between economic disparity and social well-being.

Here are a few schemes:-

- ➢ Pradhan Mantri Jan Dhan Yojana: Enables financial inclusion by providing banking access to the unbanked.

- ➢ Ayushman Bharat: Offers free healthcare to low-income families.

- ➢ MGNREGA: Ensures rural employment and livelihood security.

- ➢ PM Kisan Samman Nidhi Yojana: Provides financial assistance to farmers.

Strengthening National Security and Defence

A strong and well-equipped defense system is essential for national sovereignty and safety. The government utilizes tax revenue to maintain and upgrade the Indian Army, Navy, and Air Force. Investments in border security, intelligence operations, and defense technology rely heavily on taxpayer contributions.

Tax revenues have made the procurement of advanced fighter jets like Rafale and the modernization of the armed forces possible.

Supporting Education and Healthcare

Access to quality education and healthcare is a fundamental right of every citizen. Tax revenue ensures the establishment and maintenance of government schools, universities, hospitals, and healthcare centers.

Example:

➢ **Mid-Day Meal Scheme:** Provides nutritious food to school children, improving both education and health.

➢ **AIIMS & Government Hospitals:** Offer medical treatment to citizens at subsidized rates or free of cost.

➢ **COVID-19 Vaccination Drive:** A nationwide initiative made possible through public funding.

Driving Economic Stability and Growth

Taxes help the government manage inflation, control public debt, and ensure economic stability.

Revenue from taxes is used to subsidize essential commodities such as fuel and fertilizers, support industries, and provide financial relief during economic downturns.

The introduction of the Goods and Services Tax (GST) has streamlined India's taxation system, reducing tax evasion and increasing revenue collection for national development.

Encouraging Financial Transparency and Compliance

Filing Income Tax Returns (ITR) is not just about paying taxes but also about ensuring financial credibility.

It helps individuals and businesses obtain loans, visas, and business opportunities while maintaining compliance with the law.

Businesses and individuals with a clear tax record find it easier to obtain loans, expand operations, and secure government contracts.

Promoting Social Equity and Inclusivity

India follows a progressive tax system, ensuring that higher-income groups contribute more to the economy.

This revenue is then utilized for welfare schemes, creating a more balanced society and reducing income disparity.

Example:

- ➢ The **One Nation, One Ration Card Scheme** ensures food security for migrant workers and economically weaker sections.

- ➢ Subsidies on essential services help uplift the underprivileged.

Summary

Let us summarise this in a nutshell. Paying taxes is more than just a financial obligation; it is a direct contribution to nation-building. It funds infrastructure, strengthens national security, provides education and healthcare, and ensures economic stability. Taxes play a crucial role in shaping a prosperous and self-reliant India. As responsible citizens, we must recognize that our contributions help create a better future for ourselves and future generations. After all, a strong nation is built on the active participation of its people.

"When you pay taxes, you invest in the growth of your nation."

Now, since we understand that paying taxes helps us contribute to nation-building, let us bust some myths about income tax laws.

MYTH: ITR FILING OPTIONAL IF NO TAX IS OWED

Income Tax Return Filing is Optional if No Tax is Owed- A Myth or Reality?

Many individuals believe that if their taxable income falls below the prescribed threshold, they are not required to file an Income Tax Return (ITR). While this is technically true in some cases, multiple benefits and exceptions make ITR filing essential, even when no tax is owed.

1. Understanding the Legal Requirement

According to the Income Tax Act 1961, individuals whose total income does not exceed the basic exemption limit are not mandatorily required to file an ITR. For Assessment Year (AY) 2025-26, the exemption limits are:

Age	Basic Exemption limit (old Regime)	Basic Exemption Limit (New Regime)
Below 60	₹ 2,50,000	₹ 3,00,000
60 years or more but below 80 year	₹ 3,00,000	₹ 3,00,000
80 years and above	₹ 5,00,000	₹ 3,00,000

If a person's total income before deductions and exemptions does not exceed these limits, they may not be legally bound to pay an ITR.

2. Cases Where ITR Filing is Mandatory Even if No Tax is Owed

There are specific situations where filing an ITR is mandatory, **even if an individual has no tax liability:**

a) If you are a company or a firm

If you are a company or a firm, filing an ITR (income tax return) is mandatory regardless of your profit or loss.

b) If TDS has been deducted

Suppose Tax Deducted at Source (TDS) has been deducted from salary, fixed deposits, or professional earnings, but the taxable income is below the exemption limit.

In that case, an ITR must be filed to claim a refund.

c) If One Owns Foreign Assets or Earns Foreign Income

Individuals who own **foreign bank accounts, foreign stocks, foreign assets, or earn foreign income** must compulsorily file an ITR, irrespective of their taxable income.

d) If you have spent a High Amount on Certain Transactions

If a person has made high-value transactions, filing an ITR is mandatory, even if they have no taxable income

These include:

- ➢ Spending ₹ 2 Lakh + on foreign travel

- ➢ Depositing ₹ 50 Lakh + in a savings account

- ➢ Depositing ₹ 1 Crore + in a current account

- ➢ Having a total electricity bill of ₹ 1 Lakh + in a year

e) If you Are Carrying Forward Losses

An ITR must be filed even if no tax is payable to carry forward business losses or capital losses for future tax benefits.

f) If You Are a Director in a Company

If a person holds the position of Director in a company or has unlisted equity shares, they must file an ITR regardless of income.

g) If You Have Income from Crypto or Virtual Digital Assets (VDAs)

As per the latest tax laws, even if crypto earnings are below the taxable limit, transactions must be reported in the ITR.

h) Claiming tax exemption on capital gain

As per the Income-tax Act, an individual can claim exemption on capital gains through sections 54, 54B, 54D, 54EC, 54F, 54G, 54GA, or 54GB by filing an ITR.

The ITR filing is mandatory to claim the above exemptions.

3. Benefits of Filing an ITR Even when not Mandatory

Even when ITR filing is not compulsory, it offers several benefits: Proof of Income for Loans & Credit Cards- Banks and financial institutions require ITR to approve home loans, car loans, and credit cards.

Visa Processing – Many countries require ITR proof for visa applications.

Avoiding Tax Notices – Filing an ITR ensures compliance and reduces the risk of receiving tax department notices.

Higher Life Insurance Coverage – Some insurers require ITR records for high-value life insurance policies.

Building Financial History – Helps in wealth planning, investment approvals, and government tenders.

Conclusion

The belief that "Income Tax Return filing is optional if no tax is owed" is only partially true. While individuals below the exemption limit are not legally required to file, many exceptions and benefits make filing an ITR a smart financial decision.

It enhances credibility, facilitates refunds, and ensures compliance with tax regulations.

Thus, even if no tax is payable, filing an ITR is highly recommended for financial security and future benefits.

MYTH: ITR FILING ATTRACTS TAX SCRUTINY AND RAIDS

Many taxpayers believe that filing an **Income Tax Return(ITR)** increases the risk of attracting unwanted attention from the tax authorities, leading to scrutiny or, in extreme cases, a tax raid. Although widespread, this fear is largely unfounded. The truth is that filing an ITR does not automatically trigger scrutiny, and it certainly does not invite a tax raid unless there are clear signs of tax evasion or financial irregularities.

In this chapter, we will explore the difference between scrutiny and tax raids, examine the real reasons behind scrutiny selection, and debunk the notion that honest tax compliance leads to trouble.

Understanding Tax Scrutiny vs. Tax Raid

Before addressing the myth, it is important to differentiate between two distinct actions by the Income Tax Department:

Tax Scrutiny – A standard process where the tax department verifies the accuracy of the return filed. It is conducted through a formal notice under Section 143(2) of the Income Tax Act and does not mean wrongdoing. It is merely a check to ensure correctness. The department does this in order to ensure there is no loss of revenue to the government and that the return file is correct.

Tax Raid (Search & Seizure) – A more serious enforcement action under Section 132, where tax officers physically search a taxpayer's premises based on credible evidence of tax evasion, undisclosed income, or illegal financial activities.

Survey(Section 133A) – A softer version of a raid, often conducted at business premises to verify books of accounts.

The mere act of filing an ITR does not lead to scrutiny or a raid. Instead, scrutiny is triggered by specific red flags that indicate possible misreporting or undisclosed income.

Why Does Filing an ITR Not Increase Scrutiny?

One of the biggest misconceptions is that filing an ITR increases the risk of being scrutinized. However, in reality, 99% of tax returns are processed automatically without human intervention due to advancements like faceless assessment and artificial intelligence (AI)-based selection. The selection of scrutiny cases is based on predefined parameters, not merely the act of filing an ITR.

Key Reasons Why Scrutiny Happens

Mismatch in Reported Income—If the income declared in the ITR does not match the details in Form 26AS, AIS (Annual Information Statement), or TDS records, it may lead to scrutiny.

High-Value Transactions Without Justification – Large **cash deposits, frequent stock trading, luxury property purchases, or**

crypto currency transactions may trigger tax scrutiny if they seem inconsistent with declared income.

Claiming Unusually High Deductions – If an individual earning ₹ 5 Lakh claims ₹ 4.5 Lakh in deductions under Section 80C, 80D, or HRA, the tax department may conduct a routine verification.

Foreign Income and Assets - If an individual has foreign bank accounts, properties, or investments but fails to disclose them, a tax notice may result.

Business Loss Claims - Repeatedly declaring business losses to avoid tax liability may invite scrutiny to check the genuineness of transactions.

Thus, scrutiny is based on data analytics and risk profiling, not just because a taxpayer has filed a return.

Does Filing ITR Increase the Risk of a Tax Raid?

No, filing an ITR does not lead to a tax raid.

A tax raid is an extreme step taken only in cases where the Income Tax Department has solid evidence of:

➢ **Concealment of high-value assets**

➢ **Undisclosed foreign bank accounts or properties**

➢ **Large-scale tax evasion**

➢ **Benami transactions (property held under a false name)**

For instance, a salaried professional who earns ₹ 15 Lakh per year and files regular ITRs is not at risk of a tax raid. However, a businessperson consistently showing low profits but living a lavish lifestyle – owning luxury cars, multiple properties, and making heavy cash transactions – may attract scrutiny or a raid.

In short, a tax raid is not triggered by filing an ITR but rather by evidence of financial misconduct.

Why Filing ITR is Actually Beneficial

Contrary to the myth, filing an ITR provides numerous advantages:

Avoiding Future Scrutiny- Ironically, not filing an ITR when required can actually increase the risk of getting a tax notice. The tax department tracks financial transactions, and failure to file may be seen as tax evasion.

Conclusion: Filing ITR is not a Risk; it is a Responsibility

The myth that "filing an ITR increases the chances of scrutiny and raids" is completely false. Scrutiny and raids are triggered by suspicious financial activities, not tax compliance.

Instead of fearing the system, taxpayers should embrace transparent financial reporting, ensuring that they:

➢ Declare their actual income accurately.

➢ Match the figures in Form 26AS and AIS

➢ File their ITR on time to avoid penalties.

"A Well-filed return is your best defense against scrutiny."

Filing ITRs ensures legal compliance, peace of mind, and long-term financial benefits.

Cases: When Filing ITR Helped Vs. When Non-Compliance Led to Trouble

Let's examine a few real-life scenarios to emphasize further the importance of filing an ITR correctly and dispel the myth of unnecessary scrutiny or raids.

Case 1: Filing ITR Prevents Scrutiny and Ensures a Smooth Loan Approval

Kapish's Story – A Young Professional Planning for the Future

Kapish, a 28-year-old software engineer, earns ₹ 10 Lakh Per annum. Though TDS was deducted by his employer, he wasn't liable to pay any additional tax. Despite this, he diligently filed his ITR every year.

When Kapish applied for a home loan, the bank requested the last three years' ITRs as proof of income. Because he had filed his returns consistently, his loan was approved without any delays.

Lesson Learned: Even if no additional tax is payable, filing an ITR is crucial for financial transactions like loan approvals and visa applications.

Case 2: Late or Non-Filing of ITR Leads to Tax Notice

Shaina's case – A Freelancer Ignoring Tax Compliance

Shaina, a freelancer earning ₹ 8 Lakh per annum, believed that since her TDS was already deducted, she didn't need to file an ITR. She skipped filing for two consecutive year.

A few months later, she received a notice from the Income Tax Department asking why she had not filed her returns despite having a taxable income.

She had to go through a long and stressful process to submit old returns, explain her income sources, and even pay a penalty for late filing.

Lesson Learned: Not filing an ITR, even when Tax has already been deducted, can lead to unnecessary compliance hassles and penalties.

Case 3: High–Value Transactions Without an ITR Filing Triggers Scrutiny

Amit's Case- Large Deposits Without Income Proof

Amit, a businessman, deposited ₹ 50 Lakh in cash into his bank account over six months but never filed an ITR, believing that "no tax owed means no filing needed."

His bank reported the transactions to the Income Tax Department under Annual Information Statement (AIS) Monitoring. Soon, he received a notice under Section 148 requiring him to explain the source ot funds. Since he had no proper documentation, he faced intense scrutiny, penalties, and back taxes.

Lesson Learned: Large financial transactions without a corresponding ITR filing may raise red flags and invite unnecessary scrutiny.

Case 4: Filing an ITR Prevents Scrutiny Despite High Earnings

Priya's Case – A High-Income Professional with Transparent Finances

Priya, a senior executive earning ₹ 35 Lakh annually, regularly invests in mutual funds, stocks, and real estate. Because of her multiple income sources, she ensured her ITR was filed properly each year, matching her AIS and Form 26AS details.

Even though she made high-value transactions, she never faced scrutiny because her tax records were transparent, and her ITR accurately reflected her income and investments.

Lesson Learned: Higher income does not mean a higher risk of scrutiny – accurate tax reporting ensures a hassle-free experience.

Key Takeaways from These Cases

1. Filing ITR helps in financial transactions like loan approvals, visa applications, and credit card issuance.

2. Not filing ITR, even when no tax is owed, can lead to tax notices and penalties.

3. High-value transactions without an ITR filing can trigger scrutiny
    due to mismatched records.

4. Consistently filing an ITR with accurate details minimizes scrutiny
    risk, even for high-income individuals.

MYTH: HUF IS HISTORY IN MODERN TIMES

In India, one of the most effective and legal ways to save Tax is through a Hindu Undivided Family (HUF). This unique entity is recognized under the Income Tax Act 1961, allowing families to reduce their tax burden by creating a separate tax identity.

Let's explore how HUF works, its benefits, and how you can use it for tax planning.

What is an HUF?

A Hindu Undivided Family (HUF) is a family unit that consists of A Karta (Head of the family) – Usually the eldest male member.

Coparceners: sons, daughters, and grandchildren who have a right to HUF property.

Members – Other family members who can benefit from HUF income.

Who Can Create an HUF?

➢ HUF is available to Hindus, Buddhists, Jains, and Sikhs.

➢ It is automatically created when a Hindu family starts living together but needs to be formally registered for tax benefits.

How Does HUF Help in Tax Planning?

HUF Gets a Separate PAN & Tax Benefits

HUF is treated as a separate legal entity for tax purposes. This means:

➤ It gets a separate PAN and files its own ITR.

➤ It enjoys the same income tax slab rates as individuals.

HUF Can Own Assets & Earn Tax-Free Income

HUF can receive gifts and inheritances and invest in assets like property, FDs, and stocks.

➤ Rental income from HUF property is taxed separately (not clubbed with an individual's income).

➤ Tax-free gifts up to ₹ 50,000 per year (beyond this, gifts from HUF members are exempt).

➤ Capital gains from HUF investments are taxed separately, reducing individual tax liability.

Example:

A father and son both earn ₹ 15 Lakh annually. Instead of paying 30% tax each, they create an HUF. If HUF earns ₹ 10 Lakh in rental income, it will be taxed separately, allowing tax savings under lower slabs.

Double Deductions on Tax-Saving Investments

➢ HUF can claim deductions just like individuals under Sections 80C, 80D, and 80G. (80C: ₹1.5 lakh deduction for PPF, ELSS, LIC, NSC, etc.)

➢ 80D: Health insurance premium deduction (₹ 25,000 to ₹ 1 lakh).

➢ 80G: Donations to charities qualify for deductions.

Example:

If an individual and their HUF both invest in PPF (₹ 1.5 lakh each), they can double their tax savings, claiming ₹ 3 Lakh deduction instead of ₹ 1.5 Lakh.

Business Income Can Be Diverted to HUF

➢ If an individual owns a business, part of the income can be allocated to the HUF, reducing overall tax liability.

➢ HUFs can also hire family members, and the salary they receive is a deductible expense for the HUF.

HUF Can Invest & Earn Separate Tax-Free Returns

HUFs can invest separately in:

➢ Stocks & Mutual Funds – Gains are taxed under capital gains rules

➢ Fixed Deposits – Interest earned is separate from an individual's income.

➢ Rental Property – If HUF owns the property, rental income is taxed under HUF, not the individual.

How to Create an HUF?

Step 1: Create an HUF Deed

➢ Draft a HUF deed stating the family members and Karta.

➢ Get it stamped and notarized.

Step 2: Apply for a PAN Card for HUF

➢ Fill out Form 49A and apply for a separate PAN Card for the HUF.

➢ This is necessary for filing taxes separately.

Step 3: Open a Bank Account for HUF

➢ A separate HUF bank account must be opened.

➢ All income, gifts, and business transactions should be conducted through this account.

Step 4: Transfer Assets & Start Investing

➢ HUF can receive gifts, property, and investments from members.

➢ Start investing in tax-free instruments like PPF, ELSS, and real estate.

Important Rules and Limitations of HUF

HUF Income Cannot Be Easily Divided – Once an income is assigned to HUF, it belongs to the family and cannot be taken back as individual income.

HUFs Can't Be Created Just for Tax Evasion - The IT Department monitors artificial HUFs created to reduce taxes.

HUF Can't Have Salaried Income. – A salaried person cannot shift their salary to a HUF for tax benefits.

Partitioning an HUF is Irreversible – Once dissolved, an HUF cannot be restarted with the same assets.

Conclusion: Is HUF a Good Tax Planning Tool?

➤ Yes, if you have multiple income sources (business, property, investments).

➤ Yes, if you want to reduce tax liability legally.

➤ Yes, if you want to create long-term family wealth through tax-free investments.

➤ Not useful for salaried individuals with no other sources of income.

By using HUF strategically, families can legally save lakhs in taxes while ensuring financial security for future generations.

TAX RATES FOR ASSESSMENT YEAR 2025-26

In the case of Individual, HUF, AOP, BOI, Artificial Juridical Person

➢ For Individual, HUF, AOP, BOI, AJP (Resident or Non-resident)

	Rates
Total Income (NTI) upto ₹ 2,50,000 (Basic Exemption limit)	Nil
above ₹ 2,50,000 upto ₹ 5,00,000	5%
above ₹ 5,00,000 upto ₹ 10,00,000	20%
above ₹ 10,00,000	30%

➢ For Senior Citizen (Resident Individual age 60 years or more in PY but less than 80 years)

Total Income (NTI) upto ₹ 3,00,000 (Basic Exemption limit)	Nil
above ₹ 3,00,000 upto ₹ 5,00,000	5%
above ₹ 5,00,000 upto ₹ 10,00,000	20%
above ₹ 10,00,000	30%

➤ For Super Senior Citizen (Resident Individual age 80 years or more in PY)

Total Income (NTI) upto ₹ 5,00,000	
(Basic Exemption limit)	Nil
above ₹ 5,00,000 upto ₹ 10,00,000	20%
above ₹ 10,00,000	30%

Surcharge for Assessee being Individual, HUF, AOP, BOI, and AJP:

Sr. No.	Conditions	Surcharge %
1.	Total upto ₹ 50 lakhs	No. Surcharge
2.	Total Income more than ₹ 50 lakhs upto ₹ 1 crore	10% on tax
3.	Total Income more than ₹ 1 crore upto ₹ 2 crore	15% on tax
4.	➤ Remaining Total Income (Total Income excluding Special Income) more than ₹ 2 crores upto ₹ 5 crores ➤ Remaining Total Income (Total Income excluding Special Income) is more than ₹ 5 crores.	25% on tax on remaining Income 37% on tax on remaining Income

In the case of the Company

A. **Domestic Company**   **Tax Rate**

➤ Total Turnover or Gross Receipts of

   of **P.Y. 2022-23**   25%

   upto ₹ 400 crore

➤ Otherwise   30%

B. Foreign Company   35%

(earlier it was 40%)

Surcharge:	Domestic Company	Foreign Company
Total Income > ₹ 1 crore but upto ₹ 10 crores	7%	2%
Total Income > ₹ 10 crores	12%	5%

In case of a Firm, LLP, or a Local Authority

Tax Rate: 30%

Surcharge @ 12% if the Total Income is more than ₹ 1 crore.

In the case of Co.operative society, the Tax Rate

➢ Total Income upto ₹ 10,000   10%

➢ Total Income > ₹ 10,000 but upto

   ₹ 20,000   20%

➢ Total Income > ₹ 20,000   30%

Surcharge: Same as a domestic company (7% & 12%)

In all the above cases, a Health and Education cess of 4% is applicable on tax (including SC, if any).

Sec. 115BAC: Tax on Income of Ind, HUF, AOP, BOI, AJP [Amended w.e.f. AY 25-26]

New Tax Regime

Assessee	Individual, HUF, AOP/BOI (other than Co.op. society), AJP	
Tax rate	**Total Income**	**Tax rate**
	Upto ₹ 3,00,000	Nil
	₹ 3,00,001 to ₹ 7,00,000	5%
	₹ 7,00,001 to ₹ 10,00,000	10%
	₹ 10,00,001 to ₹ 12,00,000	15%
	₹ 12,00,001 to ₹ 15,00,000	20%
	Above ₹ 15,00,000	30%
	Special Income (u/s 111A, 112, 112A, etc.) shall be taxable @ Special rates.	

Surcharge & cess	➢ A surcharge will be @ 10%/15%/25% depending on the Total Income of the assessee. In this case, 37% surcharge is not applicable even with a Total Income > ₹ 5 crores. ➢ Health & Education cess shall always be @ 4%.

Special Tax Rates(Detailed in Capital Gain Chapter)

EXEMPT INCOME

Gifts and Inheritance (Section 56(2)(x))

A) Tax-Free Gifts

Gifts are exempt from Tax if received:

➤ From relatives (parents, spouse, siblings, etc.)

➤ On Marriage

➤ Under a Will or inheritance

Taxable if: Gifts from non-relatives exceed ₹ 50,000 in a year.

Example:

➤ If Deepika's father gifts her ₹ 5 Lakh, it is fully exempt.

➤ If a friend gifts her ₹ 70,000, the entire amount becomes taxable.

Inheritance

Any amount received as inheritance is fully tax-free.

Example: Sheenam inherits 50 lakhs from her grandfather. Since this is an inheritance, it is not taxable:

Scholarships for Education

➢ Any amount received as a scholarship for education is fully exempt from Tax.

➢ The exemption applies irrespective of the scholarship amount.

Example:

Megha receives a ₹ 2 lakh scholarship for higher studies. She does not have to pay Tax on it.

Relative

A. In the case of an Individual

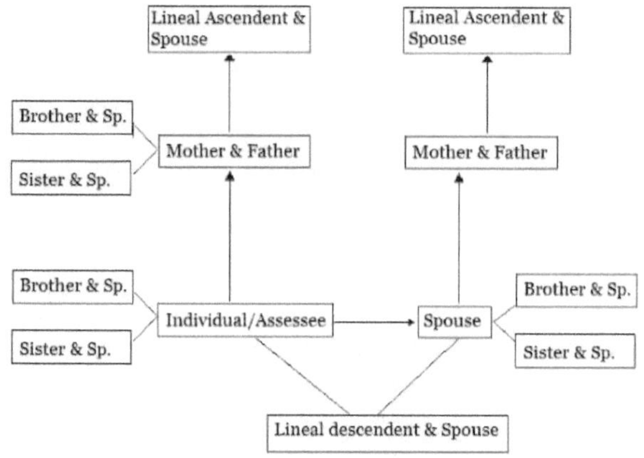

Agriculture Income

It is exempt from Tax if it's from agricultural land in India.

Agriculture income means:-

a)   Rent from agricultural land (used for agricultural purposes).

b) Income from the sale of agricultural produce.

c) Rent from a house located in a rural area (use as a dwelling house, storehouse).

d) Income from nursery, sampling, and seedling.

It is exempt, but the Income Tax Act **indirectly collects tax** on agricultural income.

If your total income is from agriculture alone, and there is no income from any other business or source, then the entire income is exempt from tax. However, if, along with agricultural income, you also have income from other sources, then the government levies tax. The method of calculation is given below. Once check

Method of partial integration:-

Applicability: Applicable only to individuals, HUF, AOP, BOI, and AJP, and not applicable to firms and companies.

Minimum agricultural income:- Should exceed ₹ 5000

Other Income :- Should exceed ₹ 250000

Step 1:- Agricultural Income+ Non Agricultural Income

Step 2:- tax on step 1

Step 3:- Agricultural Income + Basic Exemption Limit

Step 4:- tax on step 3

Step 5: Differences of tax [Step 2- Step 4]

Step 6:- Add Surcharge/ less rebate, Add HEC

Step 7:- Final Tax Liability.

Agriculture Land

There are two types of agricultural land

1. Urban

2. Rural

Urban Area

a) Any area (municipality, cantonment board, etc.) that has a population of 10000 or more.

b) In the following area within the distance, measured aerially

The shortest distance from the area referred to in point (a)	Population according to the last census
upto 2 kms	>10,000 upto 1,00,000
upto 6 kms	>1,00,000 upto 10,00,000
upto 8 kms	>10,00,000

Note:

- Rural Area means an Area that is not an Urban Area.

- There is no tax on the sale of rural agricultural land.

PROFIT & GAIN FROM BUSINESS OR PROFESSION

Any profit or gain of any Business/Profession.

The tax liability of a business depends on its legal structure. Choosing the right structure can significantly impact tax savings.

Business Type	Tax Rate (AY 2025-26)	Best For
Sole Proprietorship	Same as individual tax slabs	Small business, freelancers
Partnership Firm	30% Flat + 12% surcharge (if income > ₹ 1 Crore)	Small to medium businesses
LLP (Limited Liability Partnership)	30% flat +12% surcharge (if income > ₹ 1 Crore)	Professional firms, consultants
Private Limited Company (Pvt. Ltd.)	22% (New tax regime)	Growth-oriented businesses
One Person Company (OPC)	22% (New tax regime)	Solo entrepreneurs wanting limited liability

If business profits exceed ₹ 10 Lakh, incorporating as a Pvt. Ltd. or LLP can help save taxes compared to a sole proprietorship.

Optimize Business Expenses to Reduce Taxable Income

Under Section 37(1), businesspersons can deduct all expenses incurred for business purposes from their income, reducing taxable profits.

Key Deductible Expenses

➤ Office Rent & Utilities – If you rent an office, the full rent is deductible.

➤ Salaries & Wages – Employee salaries, bonuses, and incentives reduce taxable income.

➤ Depreciation on Assets (Section 32) – Depreciation on machinery, vehicles, and office equipment can be claimed.

➤ Travel & Accommodation – If travel is business-related, flights, hotels, and local transport expenses are deductible.

➤ Marketing & Advertising Costs – Expenses on digital ads, billboards, social media, and newspapers are fully deductible.

➤ Professional Fees – Fees paid to CA, lawyers, consultants, and tax advisors are deductible.

➤ Internet & Phone Bills – If used for business, these are fully deductible.

Chain Deductions and Exemptions

1. **Dedication for Business Loans (Interest Payment – Section 36(1)(iii))**

- Interest on business loans, working capital loans, and overdrafts is fully deductible.

- Helps reduce taxable income significantly.

Section 36(1) (iii): Interest on Loan

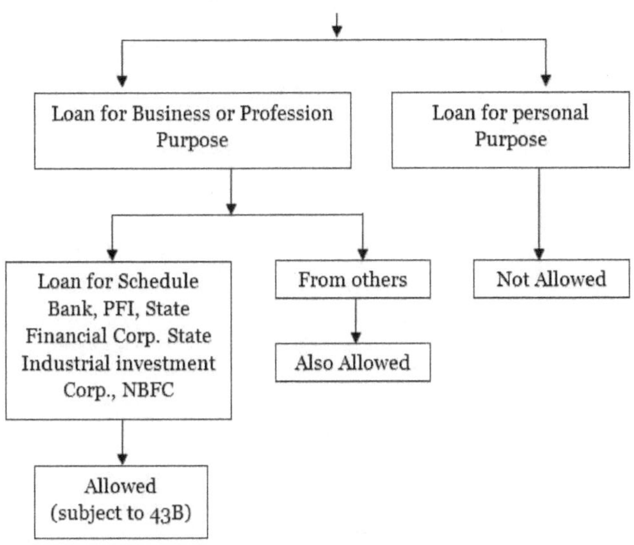

Presumptive Taxation Scheme (Section 44AD, 44ADA, 44AE)

For Small Businesses, freelancers, and transporters, the government offers simplified taxation with minimal compliance.

Scheme	Eligible Businesses	Taxable Income Considered	Turnover Limit
44AD	Small businesses	8% (if cash receipts) or 6% (if digital receipts) of turnover	Up to ₹ 3Crore

44ADA	Professionals (Doctors, Cash, Consultants)	50% of gross receipts	Up to ₹ 75 Lakh
44AE	Transporters (Goods Carriers)	₹ 1,000 per ton per month for heavy vehicles (exceeding 12000 kg) or 7500/- per month for other vehicles	Up to 10 vehicles

Example:

A consultant earning ₹ 50 lakh can opt for 44ADA and declare ₹ 25 lakh as taxable income.

(50% of revenue) saving on taxes.

Section 32 Depreciation

Conditions to claim depreciation

(i)   The asset should be used for business/professional purposes (active or passive).

(ii) Assessee should be the Owner of such asset (wholly or partly).

Classification of Depreciable Assets

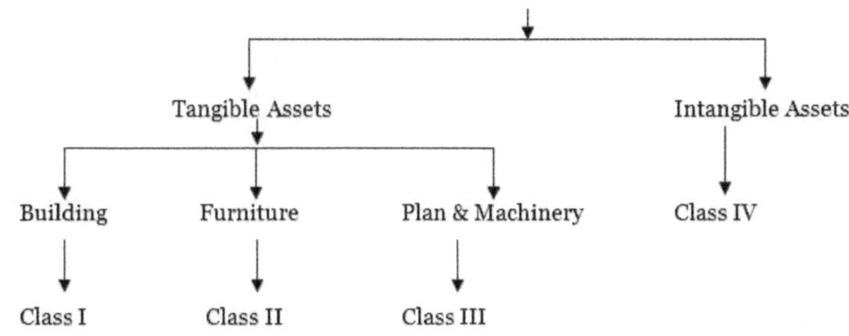

Rates of Depreciation (WDV Method) (Block of Asset system)

S. No.	Assets	Rate
1	Building (Includes roads, bridges, wells, and tube wells), Temple, (i) Residential use (except hotels) (ii) Other use (iii) Temporary or Wooden Structure	 5% 10% 40%
2	Furniture & Fittings (include electrical fittings like fans, wires, switches etc.)	10%
3	Plant & Machinery (i) Motor Vehicles - Acquired & put to use between 23.08.19 to 31.03.20 (ii) Motor Vehicles (Lorries, buses, taxis) used in Hire Business - Acquired & put to use between 23.0819 to 31.03.20 (iii) Ships, Vessels, Speed Boats (iv) Aeroplanes, Aeroengines (v) Computer & Computer software (vi) Books (include annual publication or used in libraries) (vii) Pollution Control Equipment's	 15% 30% 30% 45% 20% 40% 40% 40% 40%

	(viii) Windmills & its equipment installed before 01/04/14	15%
	- Windmills &their equipment installed on or after 01/04/14	40%
	(ix) Renewable Energy Devices (including E-Vehicles)	40%
	(x) Oil Wells	15%
	(xi) Other P & M	15%
4	Intangible Assets	25%

Notes:

1. Mandatory to claim depreciation for all assessee.

2. Mobile phones are not computers; hence, Depreciation @ 40% is NOT eligible.

3. Intangible assets include know-how, patents, copyrights, trademarks, licenses, franchises, or any other business or commercial rights of a similar nature but other than the goodwill of business and profession.

4. The depreciation rate for computer accessories,such as UPS, printers, scanners, etc., is 40%.

5. Depreciation is allowed when the asset is actually put to use & not ready for use.

6. As per Sec. 43(3),the plant includes ships, vehicles, books, scientific apparatus and surgical equipment used for business or profession but does not include Tea bushes, livestock, buildings, furniture.

WDV of Block of Assets

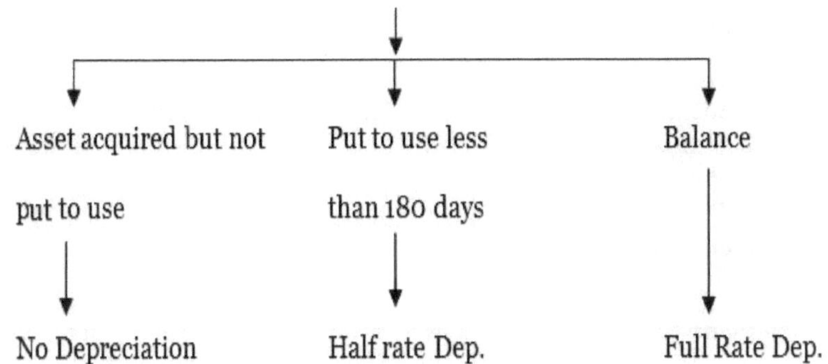

Sec. 40A(3): Cash payment > ₹ 10,000 to single person in a single Day

Suppose the assessee makes payment for any expenditure to any single person other than by A/c Payee Cheque or Demand Draft or which is more than ₹ 10,000 in a single day.In that case, such expenditure shall be disallowed.

Notes:

1. If payment is made to the transporter, then the limit is ₹ 35,000.

2. If the expenditure is claimed as a deduction in an earlier year on an accrual basis and subsequently paid in cash or bearer cheque, then the deduction allowed earlier shall be withdrawn and taxable as PGBP [40A(3A)].

3. If expenditure is paid by a cross cheque, then deduction is also not allowed.

Exceptions of Sec. 40A (3) [Rule 6DD].

1. Payment made to RBI/LIC/Banks/Govt.

2. Payment made through NEFT/RTGS/Debit card/ECS/Credit Card /UPI/BHIM.

3. Payments by book entry (adjustment).

4. Payment to producers of agricultural products, forest products, poultry products, fish products, live stock, etc.

5. Payment is made when the banking facility is not available.

Sec. 44AB: Compulsory Audit of books of accounts

The following persons are required to furnish an audit report one month before the due date for filing ROI u/s 139(1) in a prescribed form (3CA/3CB/3CD).

Specified profession	Business
G.R > ₹ 50 Lac	T.O./G.R.> ₹ 1 Crore In case of business, T.O. Limit shall be ₹ 10 Crores instead of ₹ 1 Crore if: (i) *Cash receipts out of total receipts is upto 5% during the PY and (ii) *Cash payment out of total payments is upto 5% during the PY.
Special Cases	
* Assessee claiming lower income u/s 44AD or 44ADA and NTI> Basic exemption * Assessee claiming lower income u/s 44AE	

➢ Non-applicability of Sec 44AB: Person declaring income u/s 44AD or 44ADA.

➢ Penalty u/s 271B: if the assessee fails to get accounts audited:

(i)   0.5% of T.O. or G.R. or

(ii) ₹ 1,50,000

Whichever is lower

'For Partnership Firm'

Sec. 40 (b): Payment of Interest, Bonus, Commission, or Remuneration

Interest & Remuneration paid by the Firm/LLP is allowed as a deduction if the following conditions are satisfied:

1. Remuneration is paid only to the working partner.

2. The Partnership deed should authorize remuneration & Interest.

3. Remuneration and interest should relate to the period after the date of the Partnership deed. That means they should not be retrospective.

4. Interest on partner's capital & loan allowed max@ 12% p.a. simple interest.

5. Remuneration allowed on a Book profit basis

Book Profits (BP)

On first ₹ 6,00,000 of BP		On Balance Book profit	
(a) BP x 90%	xxx	Book Profit x 60%	xxx
(b) ₹ 3,00,000	xxx		
Whichever is higher			

Meaning of Book Profit   ₹

Net Profit under PGBP   xx

(-) Current year + b/f deprecation   <u>xx</u>

     xx

(+) Remuneration (if it is debited to P&L A/c)   <u>xx</u>

     Book Profits   <u>xx</u>

In simple terms, Book Profit means PGBP before Remuneration.

TAX DEDUCTED AT SOURCE (TDS)

1. TDS requirement arises:

(i)   at the time of payment,   or

(ii) at the time crediting the A/c of the payee, whichever is earlier

But in the following cases, TDS is deducted only at the time of payment:

(i)   Salary – Section 192

(ii) EPF Payment – Section 192A

(iii) Dividend – Sec 194

(iv) Winnings – Sec 194B, 194BB, 194BA

(v)   Maturity of life insurance policy – Sec 194DA

(vi) Compensation on compulsory acquisition of property – Sec 194LA

(vii) Cash withdrawal from the bank – Sec 194N

2. All TDS rates are fixed rates, i.e., 1%, 2%, 5%, 10%, etc., but if payment is made to NR/Foreign Co. or payment of salary, then surcharge and HEC shall be considered.

3. Sec 206AA: If the payee **does not furnish his PAN** to the payer, the TDS rate shall be:-

(i) Rate as per respective section, OR

(ii) Rate @ 20%

Whichever is higher

*For Sec 194-Q, the rate is 5% instead of 20%

Section	Nature of Payment	Payer	Payee	Rate
192	Salary	Any Person	Employee (R/NR)	Slab Rate

Section	Nature of Payment	Payer	Payee	Rate
192A	Accumulated balance of PF	Any Person	Employee (R/NR)	10%

Additional points

1. TDS is required to be deducted only at the time of Payment.

2. No need to deduct TDS if the aggregate amount of the payment is less than ₹ 50,000.

Section	Nature of Payment	Payer	Payee	Rate
193	Interest on Securities	Any Person	Resident Person	10%
194	Dividend	Domestic Company	Resident Person	10%

Section	Nature of Payment	Payer	Payee	Rate
194A	Interest other than the security interest	Any Person other than Individual & HUF [Ind/HUF required to deduct TDS if last year's T/O > Rs 1 Cr in case of business or G/R> ₹ 50 Lakhs in case of profession	Resident Person	10%

Additional Points

No TDS in the following cases

1. Interest by Bank/Co. Op. Bank/ Post Office on time deposit upto ₹ 40,000 (₹ 50,000 for Resident senior citizen)

2. Interest by any other person upto ₹ 5,000.

3. Interest on Savings Bank Account.

4.   Interest by Firm to Partners.

5.   Interest on Income Tax Refund.

Section	Nature of Payment	Payer	Payee	Rate
194B	Winnings from lotteries, crossword puzzles, etc.	Any Person	Any Person	30%
194BB	Winnings from Horse Races	Any Person	Any Person	30%

Additional Points

1.   TDS is required to be deducted only at the time of Payment.

2.   No TDS if the winning is upto ₹ 10,000 during the F.Y.

3.   If the winning is wholly in kind or it is partly in kind & partly in cash and the cash balance is not sufficient to meet the TDS liabilities, then the Payer shall release the prize only after ensuring that tax on such winning is paid to the Government.

Section	Nature of Payment	Payer	Payee	Rate
194BA	Winnings from Online Games	Any Person	Any Person	30%

Sec	Nature of Payment	Payer	Payee	Rate
194C	Contracts & Sub-contracts [carrying out any work (including supply of labor for carrying out any work) in pursuance of a contract]	Any person other than Individual, HUF, AOP, BOI [Ind/HUF/AOP/BOI required to deduct TDS, if last year T/o > ₹ 1 Cr in case of business or G/R > ₹ 50 Lakhs in case of profession]	Resident Person	Payee:- Ind/ HUF 1% Others 2%

Additional Points

1. **No TDS if:-**

➢ A single contract is upto ₹ 30,000 or

➢ An aggregate of contracts in PY is upto ₹ 1,00,000.

2. No TDS if the contract is for the personal purpose of an Individual/HUF.

3. No TDS if payment is made to a transporter owning not more than 10 vehicles at any time in the PY and who furnishes a declaration to this effect along with his PAN.

4. Cold storage charges, which involve providing a refrigeration and storage facility, shall also be subject to TDS u/s 194C as a contract charge only and not u/s 194-I (Rent).

Sec	Nature of Payment	Payer	Payee	Rate
194D	Insurance Commission	Any Person	Resident Person	5 % (10% if payee Dom. Co.)
194G	Commission on the sale of lottery tickets	Any Person	Any Person	5%(2% w.e.f. 1/10/24)
194H	Commission and Brokerage	Any Person other than Individual & HUF (Ind/HUF required to deduct TDS if last year's T/O > ₹ 1 Cr. In case of business or G/R > ₹ 50 Lakhs in case of profession	Resident Person	5% (2% w.e.f. 1/10/24)

Additional Points

1. No TDS in the above sections if the Commission or Brokerage is upto ₹15,000.

2. No TDS u/s 194H on Payments by BSNL or MTNL to their public call office franchises.

3. No TDS u/s 194H if commission or brokerage related to security, like commission to the underwriter, brokerage on public issues, etc.

Section	Nature of Payment	Payer	Payee	Rate
194DA	Maturity of Life Insurance Policy	Any Person	Resident Person	5%(2% w.e.f. 1/10/24)

Additional Points

1. TDS is required to be deducted only at the time of Payment.

2. No TDS if the maturity amount is less than ₹ 1,00,000.

Sec	Nature of Payment	Payer	Payee	Rate
194-I	Rent of P&M, Equipment, Building, Furniture & Land	Any Person other than Individual & HUF [Ind/HUF	Resident Person	P&M, Equipment -2% Land, Building & Furniture – 10%

| | | required to deduct TDS if last year T/O > ₹ 1 Cr in case of business or G/R > ₹ 50 Lakhs in case of profession] | | |

Additional Points

*No TDS if the rest is upto ₹ 2,40,000 to a person in F.Y.

Sec	Nature of Payment	Payer	Payee	Rate
194-IA	Transfer of Immovable property (other than rural agriculture land)	Any Person (Buyer)	Resident Person (Seller)	1 % of Consideration or SDV, whichever is higher

Sec	Nature of Payment	Payer	Payee	Rate
194-IB	Rent of Immovable property	Individual/ HUF (Not covered u/s 194-I)	Resident Person	5%(2% w.e.f. 1/10/24

Additional Points

➢ No TDS if rent is upto ₹ 50,000 per month or part of the month.

Sec	Nature of Payment	Payer	Payee	Rate
194J	a) Fees for professional Service (FPS) B) Fees for Technical Services (FTS) c) Remuneration to directors d) Royalty e) Non-compete fees (NCF)	Any Person other than Individual & HUF [Ind/HUF required to deduct TDS if last year T/O ₹ 1 Cr. In case of business or G/R > ₹ 50 Lakhs in case of profession]	Resident Person	10%

Additional Points

1. In the following cases, the TDS rate is 2% instead of 10%:-

   • Payment to any call center.

   • Fees for Technical service (not being a professional service).

   • Royalty paid for the sale, distribution, or exhibition of cinematographic film.

2. No TDS, if the amount is up to ₹ 30,000 p.a., a limit of ₹ 30,000 p.a., is applicable separately for each nature of payment (i.e., ₹

30,000 each for FPS, FTS, Royalty, Non-compete). No limit for director fees (TDS to be deducted mandatorily).

Section	Nature of Payment	Payer	Payee	Rate
194K	Income from UTI or Mutual Fund Units	Any Person (UTI/MF)	Resident Person	10%

Additional Points

➢ No TDS if payment is upto ₹ 5,000 in a P.Y.

Section	Nature of Payment	Payer	Payee	Rate
194LA	Compensation on Compulsory Acquisition of Immovable Property	Any Person	Resident Person	10%

Additional Points

➢ TDS is required to be deducted only at the time of payment.

➢ No TDS if payment is upto ₹ 2,50,000 in a P.Y.

➢ NO TDS if the Immovable Property is an 'Urban or Rural Agricultural Land' in India.

Section	Nature of Payment	Payer	Payee	Rate
194N	Cash withdrawal from Bank, Co.op. Bank, Post Office	Bank, Co.op. Bank, Post Office	Any Person	2%

Additional Points

- ➢ TDS is required to be deducted only at the time of payment.

- ➢ There is no TDS if the cash withdrawal is up to ₹1 Crore in a PY. If the cash withdrawal is more than ₹1 Crore, TDS is applicable only on the excess amount over ₹1 Crore. Where the recipient is a co-operative society, a limit of ₹ 3 Crores is applicable for cash withdrawals.

- ➢ If the payee has not filed a return for all three preceding PYs for which the due date u/s 139(1) has already expired, then TDS shall be deducted as follows:

    - 2% on cash withdrawals in excess of ₹ 20 Lakhs upto ₹ 1 Crore and

    - 5% on cash withdrawals in excess of ₹ 1 Crore.

Section	Nature of Payment	Payer	Payee	Rate
194Q	Purchase of Goods more than ₹ 50 Lakhs in a PY	Any Person (Buyer) whose last year T/O was more than ₹ 10 Crore	Resident Person (Seller)	0.1% of the sum in excess or ₹50 Lakhs

Additional Points

➢ In this section, TDS is required to be deducted only on the excess amount over ₹ 50 Lakhs.

➢ TDS is not required to be deducted under this section if –

- TDS is deductible under any other section;

- TCS is collectible u/s 206C [other than section 206C(1H)]

➢ In case of a transaction to which both sections apply. 206C(1H) and 194Q applies, TDS deducted u/s 194Q.

➢ In case of a transaction to which both sections apply. 206C(1)/(1F)/(1G) and 194Q applies, TCS to be collected u/s 206C(1)/1F)/(1G).

➢ If thepayee'sPAN is not available, tax will be deducted u/s 194Q at the rate of 5%.

- CBDT Clarifications:

  - GST/VAT/Sales tax/CST/Excise Duty (IDT): TDS u/s 194Q is NOT applicable to the IDT amount if it is separately indicated in the invoice. However, if an advance payment is made, then TDS should be deducted from the total advance payment, as we are not aware of the IDT amount in the invoice.

  - Purchase Return: TDS is deducted at the time of crediting the party or payment, whichever is earlier. So, at the time of purchase, the buyer had already deducted TDS. In case of a purchase return, there is no need to return the TDS amount, and it can be adjusted against future purchases from the same seller. In case of replacement of Goods, no adjustment is required.

  - The first year of Incorporation: TDS is required to be deducted only if the buyer's last year T/O was more than ₹ 10 Crores. Since last year, T/O has been nil in the first year of incorporation, so this section is NOT applicable.

  - Last Year T/o: When checking the buyer's last year's T/O, it should include only Business T/O or G/R and be more than ₹ 10 Crores. Non-business T/O is not to be counted.

Section	Nature of Payment	Payer	Payee	Rate
194R	Any benefit or perquisite, whether converted into money or not, arising from business or profession	Any person other than Individual & HUF [Ind/HUF required to deduct TDS if last year T/O > ₹ 1 Cr in case of business or G/R > ₹ 50 Lakhs in case of profession]	Resident Person	10%

Due date of payment of TDS and TCS

TDS deducted/TCS collected month	TDS Due date	TCS Due Date
During the April to February months	7th of Next month	7th of Next month
March month	30th April of next FY	7th April of next FY

Note: If TDS is deducted u/s 194-IA, 194-IB, or 194M, then it should be deposited to the government. Within 30 days from the end of the month,the amount is deducted along with the return in Form 26QB, 26QC, and 26QD.

Due date of TDS/TCS Returns/Statements

Quarter Ended	TDS Return	TCS Return
30th June	31st July	15th July
30th September	31st October	15th October
31st December	31st January	15th January

| 31st March | 31st May | 15th May |

Sec 201(1A): Interest on Late deduction or Late payment of TDS

- Late Deduction: Interest @ 1% per month or part of the month on the amount of TDS from the date on which TDS was deductible till the date on which TDS was actually deducted.

- Late Payment: Interest @ 1.5% per month or part of the month on the amount of TDS from the date on which TDS is actually deducted until the date on which such tax is actually paid.

TAX COLLECTED AT SOURCE (TCS)

What is TCS?

TCS is the tax collected by the seller from the buyer on sales.

S. No.	Nature of Goods	% of Purchase Price
1	Alcoholic liquor for human consumption	1%
2	Tendu Leaves	5%
3	Timber obtained under a forest lease	2.50%
4	Timber obtained by any mode other than under a forest lease	2.50%
5	Any other forest produce that is not timber or tendu leaves.	2.50%
6	Scrap	1%
7	Minerals, being coal lignite or iron ore	1%
8	Purchase of Motor Vehicle exceeding Rs. 10 lakhs	1%
9	Parking lot, toll plaza, and mining and quarrying	2%

ADVANCE TAX

1. Advance tax means tax paid in the financial year immediately preceding the A.Y. (i.e., P.Y.)

2. Advance tax liability shall be calculated by estimating the current year's income and applying tax rates. TDS, TCS, AMT Credit, and Relief credit shall be deducted to arrive at the Advance tax liability.

3. Assessee is required to pay Advance tax if his liability for advance tax is ₹ 10,000 or more.

Exceptions: Resident Senior Citizen does not have income under "PGBP." Shall not be required to pay advance tax.

4. Due dates of Advance Tax for all Assessees.

Due Date	Amount of Advance Tax	Important
Upto 15th June of P.Y.	Upto 15% of advance tax liability	If the Assessee opts for Sec 44AD/ADA (Presumptive- PGBP), then the due date is 15th March of P.Y. (100% of Advance tax in 1 installment)
Upto 15th Sept of P.Y.	Upto 45% of advance tax liability	
Upto 15th Dec of P.Y.	Upto 75% of advance tax liability	
Upto 15th Mar of P.Y.	Upto 100% of advance tax liability	

Interest u/s 234A, 234B & 234C

Sec 234A: Interest for delay in Return filing

Tax as per ROI	x	Rate	x	Period
[After Adjustment of TDS/TCS/Advance tax/ AMT Credit/Relief] i.e. Tax remaining unpaid on 1st April of A.Y.		[1% per month or part of a month]		[From the date after due date of ROI till the date of actual filing of Return]

Notes. However, as per the Supreme Court decision in Dr. Pronnoy Roy, credit will be given for self-assessment tax if it is paid up to the due date of return filing.

Sec 234B: Interest for non-payment/short payment of advance tax

This interest is not applicable if the assessee paid 90% or more of the Advance tax payable.

Advance Tax Short Paid per ROI	x	Rate	x	Period
		[1% per month or part of a month]		[From 1st April of A.Y. till the date of actual payment of Tax]

Sec 234C: Interest for deferment of Advance tax installments

Deferred Amount   x   1% per month or part   x   3 months for all instalments
                            of a month   except last instalment

(For the last installment, Interest is applicable always for 1 month) (16/3 to 31/3)

Sec 234E: Fee for default in furnishing TDS/ TCS Statements (Return)

For the delayed filing of a quarterly statement, the assessee shall be liable to mandatory fees of ₹ 200 per day, during which the default continues. The fees cannot exceed the TDS deductible. The fees shall be paid before filing the quarterly statement.

Sec 234F: Fee for default in furnishing return of income

Where a person who is required to furnish an ROI u/s 139 fails to do so within the prescribed time limit u/s 139(1), he shall pay, by way of fee, a sum of ₹ 5000.

However, if the total income of the person does not exceed ₹ 5 Lakhs, the fee payable shall not exceed ₹ 1,000.

Sec 234H: Fees for default in Linking Aadhaar with PAN

If the assessee links Aadhar with PAN on or after 01/04/2022, then he is required to pay the following fees –

-Link between 01/04/22 till 30/06/22s – ₹ 500

-Link on or after 01/07/22 – ₹ 1,000

INCOME FROM HOUSE PROPERTY

Sec. 22: Charging Section

Rental Income (Annual value) is taxable under the head income from house property if the following two conditions are satisfied:

1. There should be House property.

2. The assessee should be the owner of that house property.

House property means a building or land appurtenant thereto.

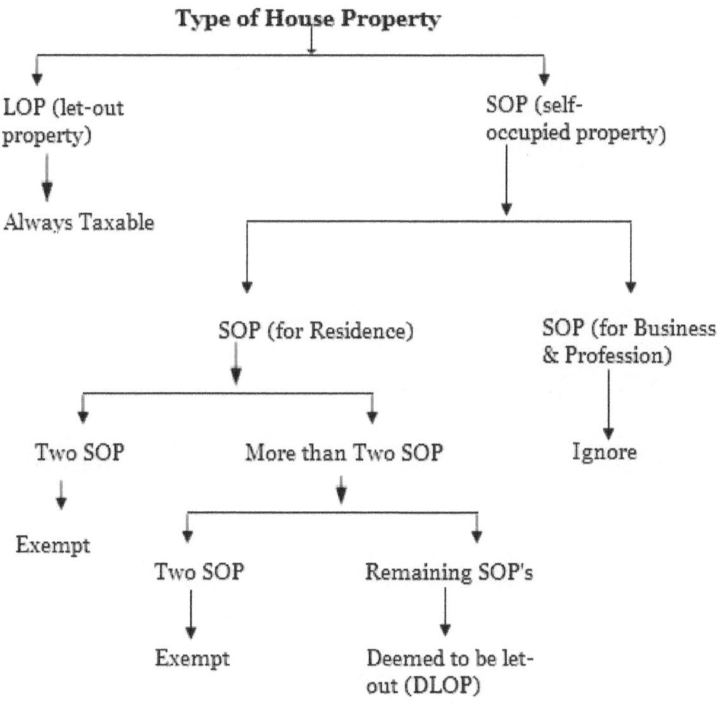

Interest on Loan

➢ Interest on a loan is allowed as a deduction if the loan is taken for house property, i.e., for construction, repair, or renovation.

➢ The loan may be taken from banks, financial institutions, trusts, friends, family, etc.

➢ Interest is allowed on a due basis [paid-Allowed; o/s-Allowed]

➢ Interest on Interest (Penal Interest) is **not allowed** as a deduction

➢ If any fresh loan is taken for repayment of an earlier loan & earlier loan was taken for house property, then the interest of the fresh loan shall be allowed as a deduction.

➢ Interest paid outside India shall not be allowed as a deduction if TDS is not deducted on such interest.

➢ Pre-construction/Acquisition interest: This refers to interest paid before the year in which construction was completed. It is allowed in five equal installments from that year.

➢ Limit of Interest Deduction

LOP/DLOP	No Limit (Full Interest Allowed)
SOP (Residence) 2 SOP ⟶	Max ₹ 2,00,000
• Special Case ⟶	

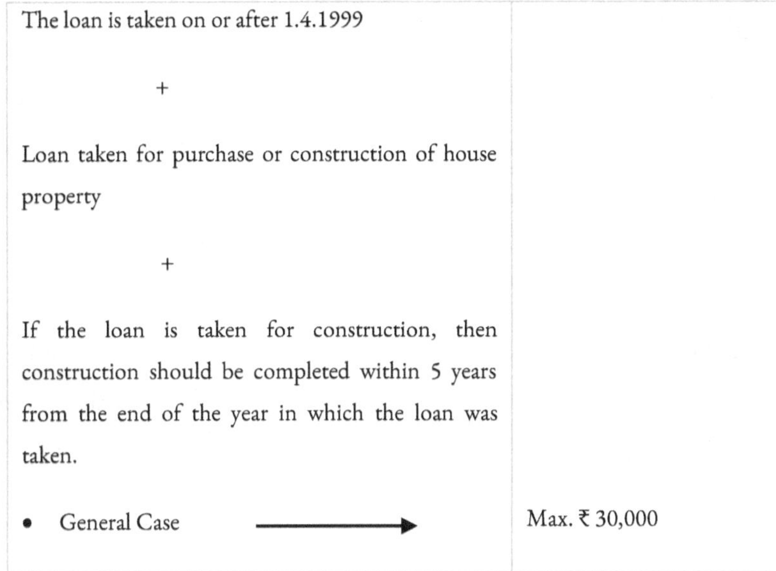

Concept of Joint Ownership

Joint ownership (co-ownership) means that more than one owner owns the property. In this case, income from house property is calculated normally and thereafter, it should be divided between co-owners in their ownership ratio.

Interest on Loan

➢ LOP/DLOP – No Limit

➢ SOP – Limit of ₹ 30,000/ ₹2,00,000 apply each owner

Sec. 27: Deemed owner

➢ If an individual transfers any house property to their spouse without consideration or inadequate consideration, then such individual is treated as the deemed owner of such property.

Exception: Transfer in connection with living apart.

➢ Suppose any individual transfers any house property to a minor child (other than a minor married daughter) without consideration or for inadequate consideration. In that case, such an individual is treated as the deemed owner.

➢ In a cooperative society, the shareholder is treated as the deemed owner of such property.

➢ In the case of Immovable property, if possession is taken in part performance of the contract, then the assessee is treated as the deemed owner.

➢ If the property is acquired under along-term lease (> 12 years), the acquirer is deemed the owner.

Some Important Notes for HP Topic:

➢ Where house property is held as stock in trade and not letout during the P.Y., the NAV of such property shall be treated as NIL for 2 years from the end of the Financial Year in which the construction was completed.

➢ If the Assessee pays tax under the default taxation regime u/s 115BAC, then Interest on a loan u/s 24(b) in respect of SOP (30,000/2,00,000) is not allowed to the Assessee.

➢ SOP exemption is allowed only in the case of an Individual & HUF.

➢ Municipal taxes paid to a foreign municipality are also allowed as a deduction if the foreign house income is taxable in India.

CAPITAL GAIN

Any profit and gain arising from the **Transfer**(Sale, Exchange, Compulsory acquisition, etc.) of a capital Asset shall be chargeable under the head capital gain in the P.Y. in which the transfer took place.

Capital Asset:

It means-

A. Property of any kind held by an assessee, whether or not connected with business or profession.

B. Any Securities held by a Foreign Institutional Investor.

Not Include:-

1. Stock in trade.

2. Moveable Personal Assets.

3. Rural Agriculture Land in India.

4. Gold Deposit Bonds, 1999 or Deposit Certificates issued under the Gold Monetisation Scheme,2015. (Interest also exempt)

Type of Capital Asset

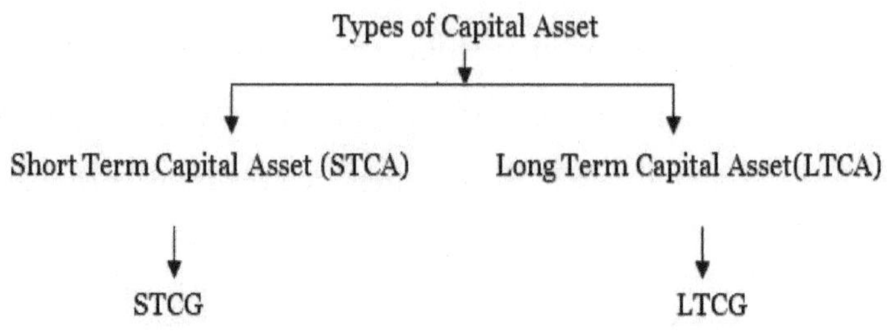

Capital Asset		Period of Holding	
		Upto 22/07/24	From 23/07/24
Part: A	➢ Security listed in the recognized stock exchange of India ➢ Unit of UTI ➢ Unit of Equity oriented Mutual fund ➢ ZCB	1 Year	1 Year
Part: B	➢ Unlisted shares (Shares not covered in Part-A ➢ Immovable Property	2 Years	2 Years
Part: C	➢ Any other Asset	3 Years	2 Years
If any asset is held for more than 1/2/3 years, then it is treated as LTCA; otherwise, STCA.			

Exempt Transfer (no Capital Gain will arise)

1. Distribution of capital assets on the partial or total partition of HUF.

2. Transfer of capital assets by an Individual or HUF under a Gift, will, or irrevocable trust.

3. Transfer of **Sovereign Gold Bond issued by RBI under Sovereign Gold Bond Scheme 2015** by way of redemption by the assessee being an Individual.

4. Transfer of capital assets under a reverse mortgage under a scheme made and notified by the CG.

(Note:- Amount of loan (either in installment or lumpsum) received by the senior citizen under the transaction of reverse mortgage would be exempt from income tax u/s 10(43).

In FY 2024-25,the Cost Inflation Index(CII) is 363.

<u>Exemption under Capital Gain</u>

Sec 54: Exemption for Residential House Property		
A	Assessee	Individual or HUF
B	Transferred Asset	Residential house property (RHP) being building & land appurtenant thereto.
C	CG on Transferred Asset	LTCG
D	Asset to be acquired	One Residential HP in India

		Note: If LTCG is upto ₹ 2 Crore, then the Assessee can acquire Two Residential HP within the prescribed time limit. This benefit of 2 HP is available only once in life time.
E	The time limit for Purchase or construction	**Purchase:** Within 1 Yr. before or 2 years after the date of transfer, and (-1+2) **Construction:** Complete construction within 3 years after the date of transfer. (+3)
F	Deposit Scheme	CGAS applicable
G	Amount of Exemption	(i) Capital Gain (ii) Cost of New Asset/ Deposit Amount Whichever is lower Note: If the cost of a new asset exceeds ₹ 10 Crores, then the amount exceeding ₹ 10 Crores shall not be taken into account for the purposes of exemption. (Added by FA 2023 w.e.f. AY 24-25)
H	Locking period on the transfer of New Asset	New Asset transferred within 3 yrs from the date of purchase or construction, then exemption claimed earlier shall be withdrawn & COA of the new asset reduced by exempted Capital Gain while calculating CG on the new asset.

Sec 54B: Exemption for Urban Agriculture Land		
A.	Assessee	Individual or HUF
B	Transferred Asset	Urban agricultural land is used by individuals or their parents for agriculture. The purpose during 2 y₹ Before the transfer
C	CG on Transferred Asset	STCG/LTCG
D	Asset to be acquired	Urban or Rural Agriculture Land
E	The time limit for Purchase or construction	Purchase: within 2 yrs after the date of transfer (+2)
F	Deposit Scheme	CGAS applicable
G	Amount of Exemption	(i) Capital Gain (ii) Cost of New Asset/Deposit Amount Whichever is lower
H	Locking period on the transfer of New Asset	Same as section 54.
I.	Notes	1. If the assessee acquired a new asset as Rural Agriculture land & if he transferred that land within 3 years, then the exemption claimed earlier shall not be withdrawn as Rural agriculture land is not a capital asset. 2. Deduction u/s 54B can also be for STCG. The condition is that land should be used by the assessee or his parents for 2 years prior to the date of transfer.

Sec 54D: Exemption for Industrial Land & Building		
A.	Assessee	Any Person
B	Transferred Asset	Compulsory acquisition of land or building which was used by the assessee in the business of industrial undertaking during 2 years prior to the date of transfer.
C	CG on Transferred Asset	STCG/LTCG
D	Asset to be acquired	New land or buildings for the industrial undertaking
E	The time limit for Purchase or construction	Purchase: within 3 years from the date of receipt of compensation.
F	Deposit Scheme	CGAS applicable
G	Amount of Exemption	(i) Capital Gain (ii) Cost of New Asset/Deposit Amount Whichever is lower
H	Locking period on the transfer of New Asset	Same as section 54.

Sec 54EC: Exemption for Immovable Property		
A.	Assessee	Any Person
B	Transferred Assets	Land, Building, or Both
C	CG on Transferred Asset	LTCG
D	Asset to be acquired	Bonds redeemable after 5 years issued, by

		(a) National Highway Authority of India (NHAI)
		(b) Rural Electrification Corp. Ltd. (RECL)
		(c) Power Finance Corp. Ltd. (PFCL)
		(d) Indian Railway Fin. Corp. Ltd. (IRFCL)
		Maximum exemption limit being ₹ 50 Lakhs within the prescribed time limit.
E	The time limit for Purchase or construction	Purchase: Within 6 months from the date of transfer of original asset.
F	Deposit Scheme	CGAS Not applicable
G	Amount of Exemption	(i) Capital Gain (ii) Cost of New Asset Whichever is lower (Max. Can be ₹ 50 Lakhs)
H	Locking period on the transfer of New Asset	If a new asset is transferred or converted into money within 5 years from the date of acquisition, then exempt LTCG will be taxable in the year of transfer/ conversion. Note: If the assessee takes any loan or advance on the security of bonds, he shall be deemed to have converted into money on the date on which such loan or advance is taken & CG exempted earlier shall be taxable.

Sec 54F: Exemption for Any LTCA other than Residential House Property

A.	Assessee	Individual or HUF
B	Transferred Asset	Any LTCA other than Residential House Property

C	CG on Transferred Asset	LTCG
D	Asset to be acquired	One Residential HP in India
E	The time limit for Purchase or construction	**Purchase:** within 1 yr. Before or 2 yrs after the date of transfer; and (-1+2) **Construction:** Complete construction within 3 years after the date of transfer. (+3)
F	Deposit Scheme	CGAS applicable
G	Amount of Exemption	$$\frac{\text{LTCG} \times \text{Cost of New Asset/ Deposit Amt}}{\text{Net Consideration}}$$ Note: If the Cost of the new asset exceeds ₹ 10 Crores, then the amount exceeding ₹ 10 Crores shall not be taken into account for the purposes of exemption. (Added by FA 2023 w.e.f. AY 24-25)
H	Locking period on the transfer of New Asset	New Assets are transferred within 3 years from the date of purchase or construction, then the exemption claimed earlier shall be withdrawn & treated as LTCG.
I.	Additional Conditions	➤ On the date of transfer of LTCA, the assessee should not own more than one residential HP and ➤ Should not purchase any other house within 2 years or construct within 3 years after the date of transfer. If the above conditions are not satisfied, then exempt CG is taxable in PY in which such other residential house is purchased/constructed.

<u>**Tax Rate under Capital Gain**</u>

Sec 112A: LTCG on the transfer of equity shares or equity–oriented units or units of business trust in excess of ₹ 1,25,000/- shall be taxable:-

(a) @10% for any transfer which take place before 23rd July, 2024; and

(b) @12.5% for any transfer which takes place on or after 23rd July 2024.

If the following conditions are satisfied:

- STT paid on acquisition & transfer of Equity shares.

- STT is paid on the transfer of equity-oriented units and units of business trust.

Note:A limit of ₹ 1,25,000/- shall apply on the aggregate of the LTCG under sub-clauses (a) and (b).

Sec 111A: Tax on STCG of certain Assets

STCG on transfer of equity shares or units of equity-oriented fund or units of business trust shall be taxable:-

(a) @15% for any transfer which takes place before the 23[rd]of July, 2024; and

(b) @20 % for any transfer which takes place on or after the 23rd July,2024,

If STT is paid on the transfer of such assets.

➢ Dedication u/s VI-A is not available against STCG taxable u/s 111A.

Other capital Gain Tax (other than referred to in 112 A & 111A above)			
No.	Particular	LTCG	STCG
A.	The transfer took place before 23rd July, 24	20%	Normal Tax Rate (slab rate)
B.	The transfer took place on or after 23rd July, 24	12.5%	Normal Tax Rate (slab rate)

Note: If a Resident Individual or HUF transfers any immovable property acquired before 23rd July 2024, and the tax calculated on LTCG at the new rate (12.5% without indexation) is higher than the tax calculated at the old rate (20% with indexation), then the excess tax is ignored. In other words, the assessee is required to pay tax at 12.5% without indexation or 20% with indexation, whichever is lower.

CLUBBING OF INCOME

Section 64(1A): Income of a minor child

The income of a minor child is taxable in the hands of the parent whose income is higher before clubbing the minor's income.

Exception: In the following 3 cases, a minor's income is taxable in the hands of the minor only:

➤ Income is due to manual work.

➤ Income is due to skill & talent.

➤ A minor child who has a disability.

Notes: If a minor child's income is clubbed in the hands of a parent, then the exemption u/s 10(32) of ₹ 1500 p.a. per child is allowed to the parent.

Sec. 64(1)(iv): Asset transferred to spouse

If an individual transfers an asset to their spouse without adequate consideration, the spouse receives income from the asset, but the transferor (Assessee) pays tax on such income.

Notes:-

1. The above provision is applicable only if the relationship of husband & wife exists at the time of transfer of the asset as well as at the time of generating the income.

2. This provision is not applicable if the asset is transferred in connection with an agreement to live apart.

3. If a House property is transferred by an individual to his spouse or minor child (not being a minor married daughter) without/inadequate consideration, then such individual is treated as a deemed owner as per Sec 27, and Sec 64 shall not apply.

Sec 64(1)(vi): Asset transferred to Son's Wife.

If an individual transfers an asset to his/her son's wife without consideration or for inadequate consideration, the son's wife receives income from the asset, but the transferor pays tax on it.

Note: This provision applies only if the relationship of mother/father–in–law and daughter-in-law exists at the time of transferring the asset and generating the income.

Sec. 64(1)(vii/viii): Asset transferred to any person for the benefit of spouse/son's wife

Suppose an individual transfers any asset to any person without consideration or for inadequate consideration for the benefit of the son's wife/spouse. In that case, income from such an asset is received by any other person (transferee), but the transferor pays tax on such income.

Sec. 60: Income transfer without transfer of asset

If an individual transfers any income without the transfer of an asset, then such income is taxable in the hands of the transferor.

Sec. 61: Revocable transfer of asset

In a revocable transfer, the transferee receives income, but the transferor pays tax.

Exception: If the transfer is revoked after the death of the beneficiary or transferee, the above provision is not applicable.

INCOME FROM OTHER SOURCES

Sec. 56(1): Any Income that is not taxable under Salary, IFHP, PGBP, or Capital gain shall be chargeable under IFOS.

Sec. 56(2) Income taxable under IFOS

➢ Dividend

➢ Winning from lotteries, puzzles, card games, etc.

➢ Interest on securities (if shares are held as SIT, then taxable under PGBP)

➢ Rent from letting out of P&M or furniture with or without building, if not chargeable under PGBP.

➢ Any sum received under the keymen insurance policy that is not chargeable under PGBP or Salaries

➢ Interest received on the compensation of the compulsory acquisition of a capital asset

➢ Gift

➢ Other income taxable under IFOS:

  - Amount received under family pension.

  - Interest on bank deposit & loan given.

- Interest on Income tax refund.

- Income from subletting of house property.

- Royalty income.

- Director sitting fee.

- Salary of MP/MLA/MLC, etc.

DEDUCTION FROM GTI

1. Deduction u/c VI-A is restricted to Gross Total income & deduction cannot be carried forward.

2. Deduction u/c VI-A is Not Allowed against LTCG, LTCG 112 A, STCG 111A & special rates of tax income.

Payment Related Deductions

Sec. 80C: Specified Investments

➤ Eligible Assessee: Individual & HUF

➤ Amount of Deduction: Max ₹ 1,50,000

➤ Eligible Investments

1. Life Insurance Premium (LIP)

    For Individuals: Self, Spouse, Children

    For HUF: Any Member

Policy issued before 1/4/12	Police issued on or after 1/4/12	Policy issued on or after 1/4/13 for person with disability (u/s 80U) or person suffering from specified disease (u/s 80DDB)

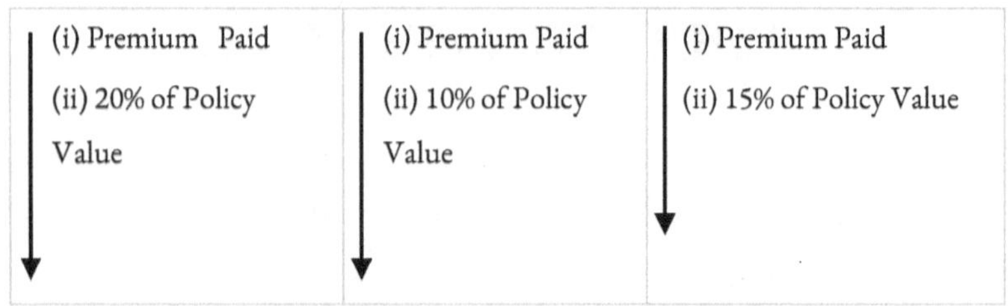

2. Amount deposited in Public Provident Fund (PPF).

   (For Individual: Self, Spouse, Children)

   (For HUF: Any Member)

3. Employee's contribution to statutory provident fund, Recognised Provident fund, or Approved Superannuation Fund (SPF, RPF & ASF).

4. The amount invested in NSC and the interest accrued on NSC.

5. Repayment of a Loan taken from banks or financial institutions for the purchase or construction of a House.

6. Fixed Deposit in a scheduled bank or Post Office for 5 years or more.

7. Tuition fees paid for the education of children. [Max 2 children for full-time education in India]

8. Deposit in Notified Bonds of NABARD.

9. Deposit in Senior Citizen Savings Scheme.

10. Contributions towards Unit Linked Insurance Plan (ULIP) or ELSS.

11. Notified units of Mutual Funds or UTI.

12. Notified Pension scheme of UTI or MF.

13. Deposit in Sukanya Samridhi Scheme A/c [For any girl child of an individual or a girl child for whom such individual is a legal guardian].

14. Stamp duty, Registration fee for acquisition of house property.

Sec. 80CCC: Contribution to Pension Fund of LIC or other Insurance company

➤ Eligible Assessee: Individual & HUF

➤ Amount of Deduction: Max ₹ 1,50,000

Sec. 80CCD: Contribution to Pension Scheme of Central Govt. /National Pension Scheme

➤ Eligible Assessee: Individual

➤ Amount of Deduction: Max ₹ 1,50,000

Sec 80CCD(1)

Salaried Employee	Other Individuals
(i) Employees Contribution (ii) 10% of salary	(i) Assessee's Contribution (ii) 20% of GTI

Sec 80CCD (1B): Additional deduction up to ₹ 50,000 shall be allowed other than contributions covered under 80CCD (1)

Example: Assessee's contribution – ₹ 1,40,000 towards NPS & GTI is ₹ 5,50,000, in this case, assessee can claim ₹ 1,10,000 (20% of GTI) u/s 80CCD(1) & remaining ₹ 30,000 u/s 80CCD(1B) or He can first claim u/s 80CCD(1B) of ₹ 50,000 & remaining ₹ 90000 u/s 80CCD(1).

Sec 80CCD(2): Employer's contribution to NPS for the benefit of the Employee

Employer's contribution is first taxable under the head salary in the hands of the Employee & then he gets deduction u/s 80CCD(2)

(i) Employer's contribution xx
(ii) 10%*/14%* of Salary xx

*14% if assessee follow default tax regime u/s 115BAC [Added by FA 24 w.e.f. AY 25-26]

*14% where C.G.or S.G.made such a contribution.

Sec 80D: Medical Ins. Premium, CG Health Scheme, Preventive Health Check-up & Medical Treatment

➢ **Eligible Assessee:** Individual & HUF

➢ **For Whom:** Individual – Self, Spouse, Parents & dependent children

   HUF – Any member of HUF.

➤ **Mode of payment:** Any mode other than cash, but payment of the preventive health check-up can be made in cash.

➤ **Amount of Deduction**

	Particular	Individual		HUF
		Self, Spouse, Dependent children	Parents	Members
A	(i) Medical Insurance Premium	Yes	Yes	Yes
	(ii) CG Health scheme	Yes	No	No
	(iii) Preventive Health Check-up	Yes	Yes	No
	General Deduction [i + ii + iii] +	Max 25,000	Max 25,000	Max 25,000
	Additional Deduction (When Mediclaim taken for Senior Citizen – Age 60 or more)	Max 25,000	Max 25,000	Max 25,000
B	Medical Exps. of Senior Citizen(Age 60- or more) & Mediclaim premium not paid for such person	Max 50,000	Max 50,000	Max 50,000
	Maximum Deduction (A + B)	**Max 50,000**	**Max 50,000**	**Max 50,000**

Notes: Aggregate payment for preventive health check-ups of self, spouse, dependent children & parents cannot exceed ₹ 5000/-

Sec 80DD: Medical treatment & Maintenance of Handicapped dependent relative

➢ Eligible Assessee: Resident Individual & HUF

➢ Amount of Deduction : (i) Normal disability ₹ 75,000

(ii) Severe disability (80% or more disability) = ₹ 1,25,000

Notes:

1. Assessee should incur expenses on medical treatment or deposit any amount for the maintenance of such handicapped dependent relative.

2. Relative Individual – Spouse, Brother, Sister, Children, Mother, Father

   HUF – Any dependent member of HUF

3. Deduction will be reversed if a dependent handicapped relative received an annuity before the death of the assessee or before attaining the age of 60 years of the assessee

Sec 80DDB: Deduction in respect of Medical treatment of specified Disease

➢ Eligible Assessee: Resident Individual & HUF

➢ Amount of Deduction:

(i)   Actual Expenses on treatment

(ii) Maximum * ₹ 40,000/₹ 1,00,000

Whichever is Lower

Less: Insurance Claim Recd.

Amount of Deduction

➤   Normal Case – ₹ 40,000

Senior citizen patient – ₹ 1,00,000

➤   Assessee should incur expenditure on the treatment of specified diseases for:

Individual – Self or dependent relative (spouse, Brother, Sister, Children, Mother, Father)

HUF – Any dependent member of HUF

Sec 80U: Deduction for handicapped Assessee

➤   **Eligible Assessee:** Resident Individual

➤   **Amount of Deduction :** (i) Normal disability ₹75,000

(ii) Severe disability (80% or more disability) = ₹1,25,000

Sec 80G: Donations

➤   Eligible Assessee: All Assessee

➤   Eligible Donations

Part A – Unlimited Category

➢ National Defence Fund

➢ P.M. National Relief Fund

➢ P.M. Armenia Earthquake Relief Fund

➢ C.M. Relief Fund & Lieutenant

➢ Governor Relief fund

➢ Zilla Saksharta Samiti

➢ National Sports Fund

➢ National Children'sFund

➢ National Cultural Fund

➢ Swachh Bharat Kosh

➢ Clean Ganga fund

➢ National Fund for the control of Drug abuse

➢ P.M. Citizen Assistance and Relief

fund (care fund)

➢ Fund for the Army, etc.

➢ P.M. Drought Relief fund – **50%**

**100%
Unlimited**

Part B: Limited Category

➢ Donations to the Govt. Or Local Authority or Approved Institution for promoting Family Planning (F)

➢ Donations by the Company to the Indian Olympics Association (O) or any other Institution for development of infrastructure for sports In India,

100% Limited

➢ Donation to Housing Development Authority (H)

➢ Donation for renovation or repair of the temple, (T)

➢ Gurudwara, Mosque, Church, etc.

➢ Donation to any Public Charitable Trust (C)

➢ Donation for Promoting the minority community in India (M)

50% Limited

RETURN FILING AND SELF-ASSESSMENT

Due Dates of Return Filing

Assessee	Due Dates
➤ Company, other than the above ➤ The person whose Books of Accounts are required to be audited under any law ➤ Partner * of a firm where the firm's Books of Accounts are required to be audited under any law	31st Oct. of AY
A person other than the above	31st July of AY

Sec 139(4): Belated Return

If the Assessee fails to file a return within the due date, then he can file the belated return within the following time limit:

➤ Before the three months prior to the end of the relevant AY (31st Dec 25 for AY 25-26)

Or

➤ Before the completion of the Assessment

Whichever is earlier

Notes: Late filing fees u/s 234F, i.e., ₹ 5,000/1000.

Sec 139(5): Revised Return

Any person who filed a return u/s 139(1), 139(3), or 139(4), if they discover any omission or wrong statement in such ROI Filed earlier, then such person can file the revised return within the following time limit:-

> Before the three months prior to the end of the relevant AY (31st Dec. 2025 for AY 25-26)

Or

> Before the completion of the Assessment

Whichever is earlier

Sec 139(8A) Updated Return (Added by FA 2022 w.e.f. 01/04/2022)

> **Updated return:** Any person may furnish an updated return of his income (or the income of any other person with respect to which he is assessable). This section is applicable from 1st April 2022.

> **Time limit:** Updated returns can be submitted within 24 months from the end of the relevant AY.

Forexample, an updated return for AY 25-26 can be submitted on or before 31 March 2028.

- ➤ **Who can submit an updated return?** Anyperson can submit an updated return, whether or not he has furnished a return u/s 139(1)/(4)/(5) for an AY.

- ➤ **When updated, the return cannot be submitted:**

1. If an updated return is a return of a loss.

2. He has already furnished updated return u/s 139(8A) for the RAY.

3. If the updated return has the effect of decreasing the total tax liability determined on the basis of return furnished u/s 139(1)/(4)/(5) or results in a refund or increases the refund due on the basis of return furnished u/s 139(1)/(4)/(5), of such person for the RAY.

- ➤ **The updated return must be accompanied by proof of tax payment and additional income tax**. It cannot be submitted unless it is accompanied by proof of payment of tax u/s 140B (i.e., tax and additional income tax).

- ➤ Computation of Additional Tax

If updated return is furnished after expiry of time available u/s 139(4)/(5) but before 12 months from the end of the RAY	25% of the aggregate of tax (+SC+ HEC) and interest as computed above
If the Updated return is furnished after the expiry of 12 months but before 24 months from the end of the RAY	50% of the aggregate of tax (+SC+ HEC) and interest as computed above

Example:

Mr. Vishant would like to furnish his updated return for the A.Y. 22-23. In case he furnished his updated return of income, he would be liable to pay ₹ 2,50,000 towards tax and ₹ 35,000 towards interest after adjusting tax and interest paid at the time of filing the earlier return. You are required to examine whether Mr. Vishant can furnish updated returns- (i) as of 31.3.24, (ii) as on 28.2.25, (iii) as on 31.5.25

If yes, compute the additional income tax payable by Mr. Vishant at the time of filing his updated return.

Mr. Vishant may furnish an updated return of his income for A.Y. 22-23 at any time within 24 months from the end of A.Y., i.e., 31.3.25. Accordingly, Mr. Vishant can furnish updated returns as of 31.3.24 and 28.2.25. However, he cannot furnish such a return as on 31.5.25.

Accordingly, Mr. Vishant is liable to pay additional income tax if he furnished his updated return on

(i) 31.3.24 – ₹ 71,250[25% or ₹ 2,85,000, being tax or ₹ 2,50,000 plus interest of 35,000]

(ii) 28.2.25 of ₹ 1,42,500 [50% or ₹ 2,85,000, being tax of ₹ 2,50,000 plus interest of ₹ 35,000]

SET OFF & CARRY FORWARD OF LOSSES

Sec. 70: Intra-head adjustment

It means loss from one source of income can be set off against income from another source of income but in the same head of income.

Exceptions:

- Speculative business loss can be set off against only speculative business income.

- Specified business loss (Sec 35 AD) can be set off against specified business income.

- Long-term capital loss (LTCL) can be set off against long-term capital gains.

- Loss from owning & maintaining race horses can be set off against income from owning & maintaining race horses.

Sec. 71: Interhead adjustment

It means a loss under one head of income can be set off against income from another head of income but in the same previous year.

Exceptions:

➢ Speculative business loss can be set off against only speculative business income.

➢ Specified business loss (Sec 35AD) can be set off against specified business income.

➢ Long-term capital loss (LTCL) can be set off against long-term capital gains.

➢ Loss from owning & maintaining race horses can be set off against income from owning & maintaining race horses.

➢ Short-term capital loss (STCL) can be set off only against STCG & LTCG.

➢ Loss from Business cannot be set off against salary.

-- For carry forward Inter-head adjustment, Not Allowed

Carry Forward & Set-off Losses				
Section	Losses to be C/F	B/F losses set off against	Time Limit	ROI on time
71B	Loss from HP	Income from HP	8 Years	No
72	Normal Business Loss	Any Business Income	8 Years	Yes
73	Speculative	Speculative	4 Years	Yes

	Business Loss	Business Income		
73A	Specified Business Loss	Specified Business Income	Unlimited	Yes
74	STCL	STCG & LTCG	8 Years	Yes
	LTCL	LTCG	8 Years	Yes
74A	Owning & maint. race horses	Income from Owning &maint racehorses	4 Years	Yes
32	Unabsorbed Dep.	Any head of Income except salary	Unlimited	No

MAY I ASK YOU FOR A SMALL FAVOR?

First, I want to thank you for reading this book. You could have chosen any other book, but you took mine, and I appreciate this. I hope you have at least a few actionable insights that will positively impact your daily life.

Can I ask for 30 seconds more of your time?

I'd love it if you could leave a review of the book. That will help me grow my readership by encouraging folks to take a chance on my books.

Keeping it straight - reviews are the lifeblood of any author.

It will take less than a minute of your time but will tremendously help me reach out to more people.

If you liked this book, please consider posting an honest review on your preferred retailer. And I'd love to see your review.

Thanks for your support.